Rocks
AND
Minerals
AND THE STORIES THEY TELL

Rocks
AND
Minerals
AND THE STORIES THEY TELL

by Robert Irving

**Illustrated by Ida Scheib
and with photographs**

j 552

Alfred · A · Knopf: NEW YORK

1 9 6 1

L. C. catalog card number: 56–8900

© IRVING ADLER, 1956

THIS IS A BORZOI BOOK,
PUBLISHED BY ALFRED A. KNOPF, INC.

FIRST PRINTING, OCTOBER 1956
SECOND PRINTING, FEBRUARY 1959
THIRD PRINTING, APRIL 1961

Contents

Contents

List of Photographs

METAL ORES [*continued*]

Galena (lead ore)
Magnetite (iron ore)
Pebbles of hematite (iron ore)

U. S. Geological Survey

ROCKS [1]

Slate
Pumice
Basalt
Agate
Flint
Gneiss

U. S. Geological Survey

ROCKS [2]

Marble
Gabbro
Granite

U. S. Geological Survey

Schist
Sandstone
Porphyry

Ward's Natural Science Establishment, Inc.

OPEN PIT MINES

A copper ore mine in Bingham Canyon

Copper & Brass Research Association

Iron ore mine in Hibbing, Minn.

Hibbing Chamber of Commerce, Hibbing, Minn.

Glaciers [2]

Glacial boulder in Yellowstone Park
National Park Service, Yellowstone Park, Wyoming

Potholes on top of Sentinel Dome in Yosemite National Park
Yosemite National Park, California

Artificial Diamonds

A press that makes artificial diamonds. One of the diamonds
is shown in the inset
Courtesy of General Electric

A Diamond Cutter at Work in Johannesburg, South Africa

South African Tourist Corp.

Minerals for Atomic Energy

Carnotite
Pitchblende
Torbernite
Autunite
Atomic Energy Commission

Beryl
The Beryllium Corporation

Monazite
Lindsay Chemical Co.

Rocks
AND
Minerals
AND THE STORIES THEY TELL

Every Rock Tells a Story

☞ **T**HERE is a story in every rock. It is a story written without words, in nature's own code. You can learn to understand this code. Then, when you look at a rock or stone, you can read its story.

TALES OF THE PAST

The stories in the rocks are tales of the past. They tell you about things that happened millions of years ago, before there were any people to see them. They tell about mountains that were born and died, and of forests that were buried. They tell of seas that invaded the land and then dried up. They tell of riv-

ers of ice a mile high, and of giant explosions
that ripped the earth.

BURIED TREASURE

They are also stories of buried treasure. They
tell of the hiding places where gold and silver or diamonds and rubies are found. They tell of vast underground stores of the riches of modern industry, like
iron, coal, and oil. They also tell of the miracle
metals of the atomic age, the fuels of the future, uranium and thorium.

To get acquainted with the code in which these
stories are written, let's look at four common rocks
and the stories they tell.

FIRST STORY: IGNEOUS ROCKS

A BEAUTIFUL ROCK

A photograph included in the illustrations following page 86 shows carloads of granite being carried

4

from quarries in Vermont. Granite is a beautiful speckled gray or pink rock often used in buildings and monuments. If you travel through Vermont you can visit one of these quarries and see how the granite is removed. The quarry is a big open pit from which big blocks of granite have been cut for many years. The quarrymen are lowered into the pit in a large bucket that is raised or lowered by a derrick. They use steel drills to separate blocks of granite from the solid mass of rock in the ground. After the blocks are cut into smaller pieces, the derrick lifts them up out of the pit.

In one of the granite quarries the men once separated a block of granite 200 feet long, 80 feet wide, and 24 feet thick. It weighed about 65 million tons. It was cut into small pieces that weighed about 25 tons each. This big block supplied enough pieces to fill 1,728 railroad cars.

To lift the blocks of granite out of the deep quarry, the derricks have to be very tall and very strong. The masts are about 115 feet high, and they are 3 feet wide at the base. They are made of Oregon fir, and have to be carried about three thousand miles from the forests where they grow to the Vermont quarries where they are used.

The blocks that are removed from the quarry are taken to manufacturing plants where they are cut up into smaller slabs. Then they are shaped and polished. A polished surface of granite is as smooth as glass and shows all the beauty of the dark and light grains of which the rock is composed.

MELTED ROCK

The story of granite is the story of the dark and light grains that give it its beauty. These grains tell the geologist how the granite was formed. Millions of years ago a stream of hot melted rock rose from inside the earth. It pushed its way into the solid crust of the earth, but did not reach the surface.

Then it began to cool. But the layers of rock above it were like a blanket holding the heat in. So the melted rock cooled very slowly. As it cooled, the chemicals in it formed crystals. Because it cooled slowly, the crystals had a chance to grow. When the whole mass finally hardened into solid rock, the crystals were big enough to be seen as the dark and light grains that make granite such a beautiful rock. During the years that followed, the rocks lying above the granite were worn away in some places. So, although the granite was formed deep underground, there are places where we find it at the surface of the earth.

Granite is only one of many rocks that were formed when hot melted rock cooled and hardened. Hot melted rock is called *magma*. All of the rocks that were formed when magma cooled are part of one big family of rocks. Because heat played a part in the making of these rocks they are called *igneous rocks,* or rocks resulting from the action of fire.

INSIDE THE GRANITE

Granite looks speckled because it is a mixture of light and dark grains. You can see these grains as separate crystals by looking at the rough surface of broken granite under a magnifying glass. The dark grains are usually pieces of dark *mica,* known as *biotite.* The light grains are of two different kinds. One kind looks glassy and is made up of crystals of *quartz.* The other kind has a milky appearance and is known as *feldspar.* While the broken edges of the quartz crystals are bumpy and shine like broken glass, the broken edges of the feldspar show many smooth, flat faces. Biotite, quartz, and feldspar are examples of *minerals.* Just as sentences are made up of words, rocks are made up of minerals.

The biotite or mica crystals in granite are rather small. There are some rocks in which much larger crystals of mica are found. They are made up of closely packed flat sheets that you can split into

8

thinner sheets and can bend without breaking.

Quartz is the most common of all minerals. Most of the pebbles, and nearly all of the sand at the beach and in stream beds are made up of quartz.

SECOND STORY: TOPSOIL

CRUSHED ROCK

We like our roads to be as straight and as level as we can make them. So, in hilly country, road-builders sometimes cut right through a hill, instead of going over it or around it. The road-cut gives us a chance to see what the inside of a hill is like. Where the road-builders blasted their way through solid rock, a wall of rock is left standing at the side of the road. But on top of the wall there may be a deep layer of soil, with shrubs and trees growing out of it. The rock, the soil, and the trees are not accidental neighbors. They belong together, because the shrubs and trees are nourished by the soil, and the soil

9

came from the rock. The road-cut in the hill tells the story of how soil is made. There was a time, many years ago, when the hill was all solid rock. But the rock near the surface was broken into pieces, and the pieces were crushed and changed into soil.

ROCK-CRUSHERS

What is there in nature that is so powerful that it can break and crush solid rock? Strange as it may seem, it is the air. The air contains water vapor as well as several other gases. Although we think of vapor and gases as soft, they are the chief rock-crushers that can turn hard granite into powder. The process by which they do it is called *weathering*.

Water comes out of the air as rain. When it falls on a rock it flows into any cracks that there are in the rock. If, later, the air becomes cold enough, the water freezes into ice. But when water freezes, it expands. So the ice acts as a wedge, widening the cracks in the rock, and breaking off pieces.

10

SODA WATER FROM THE AIR

The soda water that you buy at refreshment stands is an acid called *carbonic acid*. It is made at the bottling works by dissolving carbon dioxide in water. Nature has its own bottling works out in the open air. There is carbon dioxide in the air, and some of it dissolves in rain water. So, after a rain, a rock is bathed in some mild carbonic acid. The acid, helped by the oxygen in the air, joins the water in attacking the rock. While freezing water breaks the rock, chemical action changes it into a powder.

Let's see what these rock-crushers do to the minerals in granite. When water and carbonic acid attack feldspar, they change it into *clay*, powdered quartz, and some salts. The salts dissolve easily in water, so the rain water gradually washes them out of the rock and carries them away. Then the clay and the powdered quartz are left. When feldspar rots in this way, it swells to a greater size. The rotting feld-

11

spar helps to break up the granite just as freezing water does.

The carbonic acid and water, helped by oxygen, attack the biotite, too, and change it into clay, powdered quartz, several salts, and an iron compound called *limonite*. The salts are gradually washed out by the rain water, while the clay, the quartz, and the limonite remain. Limonite has a yellow color, so the clay with which it is mixed becomes yellow.

The third mineral in the granite is quartz. But the water and carbonic acid have almost no effect on quartz. So while the biotite and feldspar crumble into clay and powdered quartz, the quartz of the granite remains unchanged. When the granite has rotted completely, what is left is a yellow clay mixed with sand made up of the original quartz grains of the granite and the powdered quartz formed from the biotite and feldspar.

LIFE AND DEATH IN THE SOIL

Seeds are being scattered all the time by the wind, by birds, and by other animals. After a rock has begun to crumble into clay and sand, seeds that fall on it can grow there. The plants that grow from these seeds then help the air do its work of breaking up the rock. The roots of the plants reach down into cracks in the rock. As the roots grow, they widen the cracks. The pressure of the roots is so strong it can break off big chunks of rock.

Plants help to make soil even after they die. Wood, leaves, and fruit that lie on the ground begin to rot. They are gradually broken down into a dark layer of *humus* in the topsoil. Among the chemicals produced by the rotting is carbonic acid. The acid then attacks the rock to make more clay and sand. In this way dead plants speed up the process of weathering.

THE MIGHTY EARTHWORM

The soil is mixed and changed some more by an army of earthworms. Millions of earthworms living in the ground in fields and woods eat their way through the soil. They swallow soil and change it by chemical action in their stomachs. Part of the mixture in their stomachs passes into their blood as food for their bodies. The rest is returned to the soil. Earthworms carry large amounts of soil up to the surface of the ground. In ten years they bring up enough to make a layer two inches thick over the entire surface of the ground. By loosening the earth they allow more air to get in, and this also speeds up the process of weathering.

SOIL FOR THE FARMER

Where the road has cut through a hill, we can see all the steps in the change from solid rock to rich soil. At the bottom is unbroken bedrock. Above the

14

bedrock is a layer where weathering has already begun. In this layer we see a mixture of broken rock
and sandy clay. Above this mixture is a layer where
weathering has gone much farther. In this layer all
the rock has crumbled, so it is made up entirely of
sand and clay. Above the sandy clay is the topsoil,
worked over by plants and earthworms, and enriched
with humus. It is this layer of topsoil that nourishes
the crops of the farmers.

THIRD STORY: SEDIMENTARY ROCK

SEA SHELLS IN ROCK

Several years ago I was driving through hilly country with my family on a vacation trip. It was past noon, and we were very hungry, so we were looking for a picnic area where we might stop to eat our sandwiches. We didn't find any picnic area, so we stopped at what seemed to be the next best thing. In a place where the road had been cut through a hill, there was enough space at the side of the road to park the car. From there a rough slope covered with broken rock rose to the top of the hill. Clutching our sandwiches, we started climbing up the slope to find a spot where we might sit, eat our lunch, and watch the cars go by. Then we got a close look at the broken rocks on the slope. What we saw would make even the hungriest rock-collector gladly postpone his lunch. Fossils! *The rocks were full of sea shells.* We

16

searched the hillside for the nicest-looking specimens and piled them into the trunk of the car. Then we finally settled down to eating our lunch.

One of the rocks we picked up on that hillside is shown in the drawing above. The shells in it would look natural on a beach at the seashore. They look strange in solid rock one thousand feet above sea level. The shells are proof that *this part of the*

17

land was once under the sea. The rock that contains the shells must have been formed under water.

MUD TURNED INTO ROCK

The story of this rock begins where the story of the soil ends. After rain water attacks rock to turn it into soil, then more rain water begins to attack the soil. Rain water streams downhill, picking up soil and pebbles on its way. The muddy water flows into brooks. The brooks pour into the rivers, and the rivers rush down to the sea. There the mud settles out of the water and piles up on the floor of the sea. The rain water wears down the land that is high and dry, and builds up the land beneath the water.

Millions of years ago large parts of the United States were under shallow seas. Rivers flowed into these seas and piled up thick layers of mud on the sea floor. Sea shells settled on the mud and were buried as more mud settled over them. The mud was

18

pressed down by its own weight and by the weight of the water on top of it. Squeezed by the pressure, and cemented by chemicals in the sea water, the mud was turned into a rock called *shale*. Most of the shells in the mud were ground up by the pressure. But some were preserved unbroken in the solid rock. Later the land was lifted, and the shallow seas drained off or dried up. So now the shale and the shells are found inland, high above sea level.

Shale is made up mostly of hardened clay, mixed with some tiny grains of quartz, mica, and other minerals. Because the mud from which it was formed was piled up in layers, the shale is layered and splits easily along the layers.

Because shale was formed from a sediment that settled out of the water, it is called a *sedimentary rock*. There are other sedimentary rocks too, formed from sand or stones dropped in layers by water, glaciers, or the wind.

19

FOURTH STORY: METAMORPHIC ROCK

THE ROCK WE WRITE ON

The blackboard you write on in school is probably *slate*. It is made of a flat sheet of rock that tells a story of being pushed and squeezed and heated.

The crust of the earth is made of layer on layer of rock. The lower layers have tons and tons of rock pressing down on them. So these rocks are being squeezed from the top. Some layers of rocks were also squeezed from the sides. They were squeezed so hard that they buckled like a carpet whose ends are pushed together. When shale was pushed and squeezed and made hot in this way, the minerals in it rearranged themselves. The particles of clay were turned into tiny flat flakes of mica that lined up side by side to form sheets of rock. The shale was changed into slate. Where the shale was pushed from the side, the tiny flakes of mica lined up across the lay-

20

ers in the shale. So the sheets of the slate cut across these layers. While the shale broke easily along the layers, the slate breaks easily along the faces of the sheets made by the mica flakes. The hard flat sheets of slate are used for roof shingles, flagstone pavements, and school blackboards.

Because slate was formed when shale was *changed*

21

by heat and pressure, it is called a *metamorphic rock,* or changed rock. Every metamorphic rock comes from an igneous rock or a sedimentary rock that has been changed.

Rocks and Minerals

⊂⊐ THE stories told by granite, shale, and slate introduced three families of rocks. Granite belongs to the family of igneous rocks. These are formed when hot melted rock cools and hardens. Shale belongs to the family of sedimentary rocks. Some of them are formed when layers of mud, sand, or stone are cemented and hardened. Slate belongs to the family of metamorphic rocks, which are formed when other rocks are changed by heat or pressure. Every rock belongs to one of these three families. Each rock tells its family story. But it also tells its own personal story of how and where it was formed, and how it may be used.

To read the story of a rock you have to be able

to recognize it. Every rock is made up of minerals. So, to get acquainted with the rocks, you have to learn how to recognize different minerals.

In some rocks, like shale, the separate pieces of the minerals in the rock are so small they cannot be seen with the naked eye. To identify these minerals

SHALE

the rock specialist may look at them through a microscope, pass X-rays through them, or use chemical tests. But when a mineral sample is big enough to be seen and handled, there are easier ways of recognizing it. The beginner as well as the specialist can recognize one of the common minerals by *how it looks, how it breaks,* and *how hard it is.*

24

THE SHAPE OF A MINERAL

Every mineral is made up of certain chemical elements that arrange themselves in groups to form a crystal. Each crystal has a special shape of its own. When a crystal is first formed, it is very small. As more and more of the chemical elements of the mineral attach themselves to the crystal, the crystal grows. But whether it is large or small, a perfect crystal of the same mineral always has the same shape. When many crystals are crowded together, their shapes may be partly destroyed. But even then enough of the shape may be left to be recognized. Sometimes a small crystal grows on a larger one, so a mineral sample may be a family of large and small crystals all in one lump.

There are crystals of many different shapes. Some look like bricks with smooth faces, while others look like pyramids. Some are flat like paper, and some are long and thin like needles. Some interesting crystal

25

These are crystals of

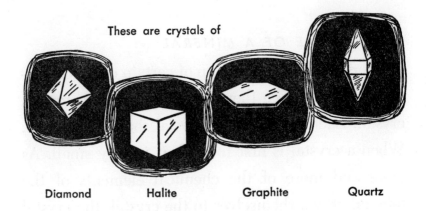

Diamond   Halite   Graphite   Quartz

shapes are shown in the drawing above. A *diamond* crystal looks like two pyramids attached to each other base to base. A *halite* crystal, made of ordinary table salt, is shaped like a cube. *Graphite*, used in lead pencils, has crystals that are flat sheets. *Quartz* crystals come to a point with six faces.

HOW A MINERAL BREAKS

The way the chemical elements in a mineral are arranged gives it an inside shape as well as an outside shape. The inside shape shows up when you break a sample of the mineral. Many minerals split

26

into pieces with smooth flat faces. These faces are called *cleavage planes*. (*Cleavage* means "splitting.") Where two faces come together they form an angle. The shape of the angle helps to identify a mineral.

Many minerals break into rough pieces instead of breaking along cleavage planes. But even some of the rough breaks have special shapes that can be recognized. Quartz, for example, breaks like glass. The surface of the break is curved, and resembles a sea shell. The kind of rough surface you get when you break a mineral is called its *fracture*. (*Fracture* means break.) The shell-like surface where quartz or glass breaks is called *conchoidal fracture*, named after the sea shell known as a conch.

MAKING SCRATCHES

To see how hard a mineral is, we rub a pointed corner of it on the face of another mineral. If it makes a scratch, it is harder than the mineral it was

27

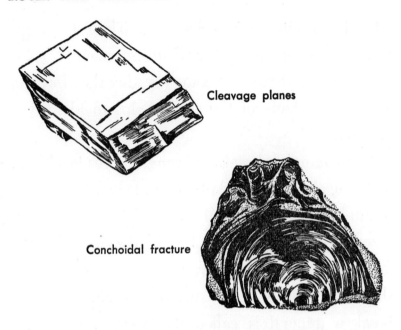

Cleavage planes

Conchoidal fracture

rubbed against. A mineral will always scratch a softer one, but will not scratch a harder one. For example, you can scratch a copper penny with the blade of your pocketknife. So the steel of the blade is harder than the copper of the penny. But you cannot scratch quartz with the knife. So quartz is harder than the steel of your knife.

To get a scale of hardness, geologists picked out ten

28

minerals and arranged them in order of hardness, from the softest to the hardest. Then they gave each one a number from one to ten. The number is the measure of its hardness. Here is the scale:

1. talc
2. gypsum
3. calcite
4. fluorite
5. apatite

6. feldspar
7. quartz
8. topaz
9. corundum
10. diamond

To get the measure of the hardness of any other mineral, you compare it with these ten by seeing which ones it will scratch. To test the hardness of your fingernail, for example, you would try to scratch each of the ten minerals in turn. Your finger-nail will scratch talc and gypsum, but it will not scratch calcite, or anything harder. So the hardness of your fingernail is between 2 and 3. It is about 2½.

You can buy a set of these minerals (including all except the diamond) from scientific supply houses or

29

from a museum of natural history. The set is cheap, and will have a triple use: (1) It will help you test the hardness of other minerals. (2) It will help you learn how to recognize the shapes of the crystals in the set. (3) It will also be a good start for your mineral collection.

You can make up your own hardness-testing set, too. For a homemade set use your thumbnail, a copper penny, and a pocketknife or a smooth flat piece of window glass. When you handle the knife or the glass, be careful not to cut yourself. Your thumbnail has hardness 2½. It will scratch talc and other stones of hardness 1 very easily. It will also scratch gypsum and other stones of hardness 2, but not so easily as it will scratch talc. It will not scratch calcite or any stones as hard as calcite or harder. The copper penny has hardness 3½. It will scratch calcite and other stones of hardness 3. It will also scratch any stones that are softer than calcite. It will

30

not scratch fluorite, or any stones as hard as fluorite or harder. The steel blade of your pocketknife has hardness 5½. It will scratch fluorite and apatite and stones as hard as they are. It will also scratch any stones softer than fluorite. It will not scratch feldspar, or any stones as hard as feldspar or harder. Window glass also has hardness 5½. After you have found and identified some common minerals like feldspar and quartz, you can add them to your hardness set. This will bring your scale up to hardness 7.

THE COLOR OF A MINERAL

Sometimes the *color* of a mineral helps you to recognize it, because some minerals always have the same color. But color is not a foolproof clue. Some minerals may have many different colors that they get from impurities that are mixed with them. Some minerals change color on the surface where they are touched by air or water. To get the true color of these minerals you have to break them open and look at the new surface that hasn't had a chance to be weathered.

A more reliable clue is given by the color of the powder of a mineral. This is called the *streak*. To make the streak, rub the mineral against the unglazed side of a piece of white tile of the kind used in bathrooms. Some minerals have a powder color or streak that is different from the color of a big piece.

REFLECTED LIGHT

Minerals reflect light in different ways. The way they reflect light is called the *luster* or shine. If they look like polished metal, they have a *metallic luster*. If they look glassy, they have a *vitreous luster*. If they shine the way diamonds do, they have *adamantine luster*. Some have a *silky luster*, others a *pearly luster*. Some look *resinous*, and others look *dull* or *earthy*.

COMMON AND FAMILIAR MINERALS

PEBBLES

Pick up any large white pebble on the beach, in a stream bed, or at the side of a road. It is probably made of *quartz,* the most common of the minerals. You can make sure by testing it. First crack it by giving it a hard blow with a hammer. If it is quartz it will break with a *rough surface,* instead of splitting along a flat surface. It may show *conchoidal fracture,* like a broken piece of glass. The broken surface will have a glassy shine or vitreous luster.

Now test it for hardness. Try to scratch it with your knife. If it is quartz, the knife won't scratch it at all. Then rub a sharp edge of the broken pebble against the blade of your knife or across a piece of glass. If the pebble scratches the knife or glass you can be fairly sure that it is quartz. Quartz is the only common mineral hard enough to scratch glass easily.

33

Most quartz is made up of crystals that are not well formed, so you can't see the shape of the crystals. This kind of quartz is called *massive quartz*. If it is white it is known as *milky quartz*. If it has a smoky yellow or brown color it is called *smoky quartz*. Some quartz is red, some is purple, some black, and some blue. The colors come from different minerals that are mixed with the quartz.

QUARTZ CRYSTALS

While most quartz is massive quartz, there are places where you can find well-formed quartz crystals. The crystals are prisms with six faces, and they come to a point. Sometimes they are pointed at both ends. If the quartz is pure, the crystals are colorless like clear glass, and you can see right through them. If the quartz is not pure, the crystals may be colored. Colorless quartz crystals are known as *rock crystals*. They can be found in the Hot Springs area of Arkansas, and near Little Falls, New York. Rock crystals are used in some radio transmitters to control the frequency of the electrical vibrations. Violet quartz crystals are called *amethysts*. Amethysts are found in Maine, Pennsylvania, and North Carolina. They are used as gem stones.

A STONE BECOMES A PEBBLE

Quartz is found in smaller or larger pieces in many different rocks. When weathering breaks up the rocks on the ground, some of the minerals in the rocks may crumble to form clay. But the quartz does not crumble. Air does not change it, and water does not dissolve it. While the other minerals crumble, the pieces of quartz in the rocks remain whole. They are scattered in the soil that is formed from the rocks.

In the springtime, melted snow and heavy rains soak the ground with water. Large amounts of water run off the hills and pour into lakes, brooks, and rivers. They loosen the soil and carry part of it with them. When the water flows swiftly, it is strong enough to carry stones as well as sand and fine clay. So, during the spring floods, many quartz stones are washed into the streams. Because they are big and heavy, they sink to the bottom. Here they are pushed along, bouncing up and down, and bumping against one another. Each stone acts as a grindstone for its neighbors. They rub off each other's sharp edges until they are all round and smooth. That's how rough quartz stones are turned into smooth quartz pebbles. Pebbles are also formed at the seashore. Here the tide and the waves pound against the beach and make sand and stones rub against each other all the time.

PILES OF PEBBLES

Quartz pebbles are often found in big piles in stream beds or on the seashore.

During the springtime, streams are swollen with water. They grow wider and deeper, flow swiftly, and may overflow their banks. Later, when less water flows into the streams, they become smaller again and flow more slowly. In very dry weather they may even dry up altogether. If you walk along a dry stream bed you find piles of pebbles in the middle, where they were dropped by the stream. On both sides of the pile of pebbles you will find piles of sand. And on the banks where the stream overflowed,

you will find piles of clay mud. The pebbles, the sand, and the mud were separated by the stream. The pebbles were dropped in the center when the stream began to flow more slowly and didn't have the strength to carry the pebbles any more. No sand or mud was dropped in the center because the stream still moved fast enough there to carry them along. Nearer to the shore, the stream flowed more slowly than at the center, so here even sand became too heavy to carry. Where the stream had overflowed its banks and formed pools of water over level land, the water hardly flowed at all. Here even the clay began to settle out, and formed a layer of mud. In this way flood waters act as a sieve separating pebbles from sand and mud.

A stream acts as a sieve even when it is not in flood. All through the years streams flow most rapidly down a steep slope. They slow down when the land they flow over becomes more level. As they slow down, they drop stones and pebbles first; then they drop sand, and they drop fine clay particles last. The stones and pebbles form layers of gravel at the foot of steep slopes. The sand and the clay are dropped farther downstream.

The restless water of the sea also acts as a sieve, separating pebbles from sand and mud. Pebbles and sand are found on the shore where the water is most active; mud is found under deep water, where the water is calm.

QUARTZ SAND

Some rocks have only small grains of quartz in them. When these rocks weather and crumble, the quartz remains as sand. The quartz sand is mixed with small grains of feldspar, mica, and pieces of other minerals. Flowing water washes the pebbles, sand, and clay out of the soil and then separates them. So piles of sand are formed near the banks of streams and on the seashore. Sand grains made of feldspar, mica, and most other minerals crum-

39

ble and are finally washed away. Quartz sand does not weather, so it remains. That's why nearly all the sand you find at most beaches is made of quartz.

Because of its hardness, quartz sand is used to make sandpaper. It is also one of the materials used to make glass.

A STONE EYE

Some quartz is made up of tiny crystals that are too small to be seen without a microscope. The crystals may be arranged in bands or layers, sometimes of different colors. Where the colored layers are arranged in rings, the rock looks like an eye, and is called *agate*. If the layers are straight, it may be *onyx*. Agate and onyx allow light to pass through them, but you can't see through them. They are used as decorative stones.

Some quartz is made of tiny crystals that are closely packed but not arranged in layers. *Flint* is an example of this kind of quartz. It does not allow

light to pass through it. Flint breaks with a sharp edge. Before men knew how to smelt metals, they made their knives, axes, and arrowheads out of flint.

FELDSPAR

Not all the large pebbles you will find are made of quartz. Some of them may be *feldspar*. Because feld-

41

spar is often white or pink, like quartz, you may at first think that it is quartz. But there are easy ways of telling quartz and feldspar apart. First, they don't have the same luster or shine. Quartz is glassy, while feldspar shines more like a piece of china. Secondly, when you break them, feldspar splits along cleavage planes, while quartz does not. Finally, although feldspar is one of the harder minerals, it is not so hard as quartz. You can't scratch either feldspar or quartz with a knife. But while quartz easily scratches glass, feldspar will make only faint scratches even when you press hard.

A feldspar crystal is shown in the pictures after page 86. Good crystals can be found at Robinson, Colorado, and Good Springs, Nevada.

Feldspar, like quartz, is used in glassmaking.

A SODA-MAKING ROCK

Another light-colored mineral is *calcite*. It is usually white, but may be slightly colored by impurities.

Like feldspar, it breaks along cleavage planes. But it is much softer than feldspar. It has hardness 3, so you can scratch it with a copper penny.

The surest way to recognize calcite is by a simple chemical test. Put a drop of vinegar on it. The vinegar and the calcite combine to make carbonic acid (soda water). Then the carbonic acid *fizzes like soda water* while bubbles of carbon dioxide escape. This will not happen when you drop vinegar on feldspar or quartz.

Calcite crystals that are colorless and as clear as glass are called *Iceland spar*. When a beam of light passes through Iceland spar, it is split into two separate beams. So if you look at something through a crystal of Iceland spar, you see double.

MICA

Mica is found with quartz and feldspar in granite. In most granite the mica crystals are tiny, and are seen as dark spots in it, like raisins in a rice pud-

43

ding. But there is one kind of granite, called *pegmatite*, that has giant crystals. Pegmatite is often found in *dikes*. A dike is a wall of rock formed when magma flowed up into a crack in another rock and then hardened as it cooled.

Mica crystals are soft flat sheets that split easily into thinner sheets. A sheet of mica is flexible, so you can bend it without breaking it. It is elastic, so that after being bent, it snaps back when you let it go. There are several kinds of mica. The common light-colored mica is called *muscovite,* because the Russians (Muscovites) used to make windowpanes out of it. The common dark mica is called *biotite.* It gets its dark color from the iron in it. You can scratch biotite with a copper penny. Muscovite is softer and can be scratched by your fingernail. Mica has a glassy or pearly luster.

Mica is mined from pegmatite in Colorado, North Carolina, New England, and the Black Hills of South Dakota. Electric currents don't flow easily through

44

mica, so it is used as an insulator in electrical equipment. The metal parts inside a radio tube are attached to a disk of mica. Some electrical capacitors have mica sheets separating the plates on which electrical charges are stored. Because mica does not burn, small flakes of mica are used as "snow" for your Christmas tree.

ROTTED ROCK

Air and water make mica and feldspar rot to form *kaolinite,* the mineral of clay. Pure kaolinite is white, but most clay is colored by the impurities in it. The crystals are too small to be seen, because clay is found as a powdery mass. It has a dull earthy luster. Kaolinite gives off an earthy odor when you breathe on it. Clay is an important part of the soil in which we grow our food. It can also be molded and hardened to make pottery and bricks.

45

THE MINERAL WE DRINK

Most minerals are solids at ordinary temperatures. We have to make them very hot to melt them into liquids. But there is one common mineral that is already melted at ordinary temperatures. This mineral is *water*. But it, too, becomes solid when it is cooled to its freezing point to form snow or ice.

In cold weather, water vapor comes out of the air in your room and settles on your windowpane to form frost. The frost is made up of crisscrossing needlelike crystals of ice. When the water vapor freezes outdoors, high up in the atmosphere, to form snow, the snowflakes grow as six-pointed crystals of many beautiful shapes.

THE MINERAL WE EAT

Sprinkle some table salt on a plate and look at it through a magnifying glass. You will find that the grains of salt are little cubes. They are crystals of the mineral *halite*.

For thousands of years people have been using clay to make pottery.

Prehistoric urn.

Egyptians of long ago stored grain in pottery jars like this.

Roman hand lamps (made of pottery) burned oil.

Ancient Chinese porcelain jar.

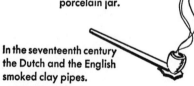

In the seventeenth century the Dutch and the English smoked clay pipes.

American Indians of the Southwest made pottery jars like this.

Dutch Delft tiles are still used to decorate fireplaces.

Halite dissolves easily in water and has the familiar salty taste for which we use it. If some halite grains are sprinkled over a gas flame, the flame becomes a bright yellow. Halite splits along cleavage planes in three directions to form perfect cubic corners.

Halite is found in New York State, Kansas, Michigan, and New Mexico. In some places it is mined, or dug up out of the ground. In other places, water is poured into wells to dissolve the salt in the ground. Then the salty water or brine is pumped out and evaporated. As the water dries up, the salt remains behind.

At Great Salt Lake in Utah, salt crystals are forming all the time as the water of the lake evaporates.

HOMEMADE CRYSTALS

One way of getting a good large halite crystal is to make one yourself. Boil a cup of water and, while it is hot, dissolve as much salt in it as it will hold. Let

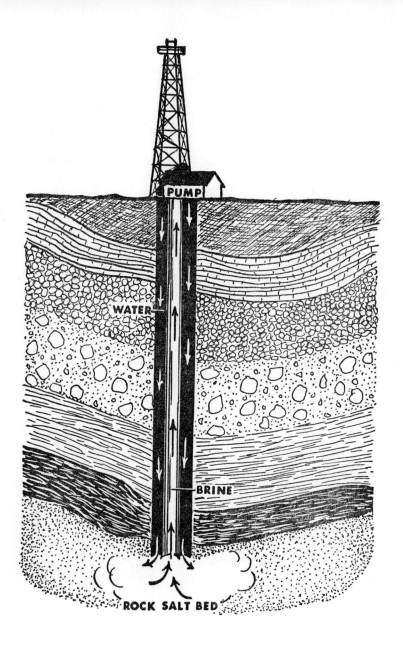

PUMP

WATER

BRINE

ROCK SALT BED

the excess settle to the bottom. Then slowly pour the clear liquid into a shallow dish. You can filter it as you transfer it to the shallow dish by pouring it through filter paper placed in the mouth of a fun-

nel. (Several thicknesses of ordinary cleansing tissue make a good filter paper.) Now cover the dish with paper and let it stand for several days. As the water evaporates, halite crystals will form and grow. Small crystals will grow on larger ones to make interesting shapes. Some of the crystals will look like groups of skyscraper buildings in a big city. Look at the dish from time to time and remove the smaller crystals. This will give the larger ones a chance to grow even larger. You can add fresh salt solution over and over again to keep the crystals growing. To prevent small crystals from climbing up the side of the dish, rub some Vaseline around the inside of the dish above the surface of the solution.

IGNEOUS ROCKS

NEW ROCKS ON HAWAII

In March 1955 cracks appeared in the ground on the southeastern shore of the island of Hawaii. Hiss-

51

ing steam rose out of the cracks. Then red-hot melted rock flowed out of the cracks and spread over the ground. As soon as the hot melted rock came out of the ground, it began to cool. As it cooled, it hardened to form a new layer of igneous rock on the slopes of the island.

Hot melted rock that rises out of the ground into the open air is called *lava*. A place where lava erupts, or bursts out of the ground, is called a *volcano*, named after the ancient Roman god of fire, Vulcan. There are two volcanoes on the island of Hawaii. The one that erupted in 1955 is called Kilauea. Its sister volcano, Mauna Loa, had erupted five years earlier. The whole island of Hawaii is made up of layers of hardened lava from these two volcanoes, piled up to a height of 14,000 feet above the sea.

When lava cools off, if crystals form in it at all, they form so fast that they don't have time to grow. So the rock that is formed is made up of closely packed tiny crystals, or is *fine-grained*. The rock usu-

52

ally formed by cooling lava is *basalt*. Among the minerals in basalt are *pyroxene* and *olivine,* two dark-colored minerals that contain iron and magnesium. Basalt has feldspar in it, too, but it has no quartz. Because of the pyroxene and olivine in it, basalt is colored gray or black. The island of Hawaii is nearly all basalt.

NATURAL GLASS

Sometimes lava cools so very rapidly that there is no time for crystals to form at all. Then it hardens into a rock that looks like glass. In fact it is glass, except that it is made by nature instead of by man. If the lava that makes the glass is the same as the lava that makes basalt, then the glass is called *basalt glass*. But if the lava is mostly melted feldspar, with only small amounts of pyroxene or olivine in it, then the glass is called *obsidian*. Basalt glass is jet-black. Obsidian is usually black, but may also be red or brown.

53

WHIPPED LAVA

We make meringue by whipping the white of an egg into a froth. As we whip the egg-white, we push bits of air into it. The egg-white is sticky and traps the air, so it cannot escape. Pretty soon we have a mass of air bubbles surrounded by thin films of egg-white.

Volcanoes whip lava the way we whip egg-white. There are hot gases that pour out of a volcano with the lava. Sometimes these gases are trapped in the sticky lava and form bubbles in it. When the lava comes out into the open air, the bubbles grow and blow up to form a bubbly froth. When the froth cools and hardens, it forms a rock called *pumice*. Because pumice is so full of bubbles it weighs very little. In fact, it is so light that it *floats in water*.

VOLCANOES OF THE PAST

Basalt and obsidian are both found in the western part of the United States. They show that volcanoes must have been active there in the past. A long time ago great streams of lava flowed out of cracks in the ground and hardened on the surface. Later streams of lava flowed over the rock formed from earlier ones. Big piles of basalt grew up, covering large areas, and reaching great heights. In Idaho, Oregon, and Washington, about 200,000 square miles were covered. In some places the basalt is 2,000 feet thick.

PILLOW LAVA

There are many island volcanoes in the Pacific Ocean. Sometimes lava from one of these volcanoes flows into the sea. The water boils and hisses, sending up clouds of steam. Meanwhile the lava breaks up, and hardens into rounded lumps of rock known as *pillow lava*. The inside of a pillow lava is basalt. But the surface of the pillow, where it was chilled

55

quickly by the water, is a layer of glass. Pillow lavas are found in Washington and Oregon. They show that when the volcanoes were active there, much of the land was covered by shallow seas.

TWO FAMILIES

There are two families of igneous rocks. In one family, the rocks have only small crystals or no crystals at all. This is because they hardened quickly from lava that flowed out of the ground. Basalt, obsidian, and pumice belong to this family. Because they come from volcanoes, they are called *volcanic rocks*. But there are other igneous rocks, like granite, which have large crystals in them. These rocks were formed from *magma*, the hot melted rock that never came out of the ground, but cooled underground. The crystals in these rocks are large because the magma was covered by a blanket of rock, so it cooled off slowly, and the crystals had time to grow. These igneous rocks that were formed under the ground are

56

called *plutonic rocks*. They are named after Pluto, the Roman god of the underworld.

Granite is the plutonic rock with the lightest colors. New England granite is gray. Canadian granite is pink. Another light-colored plutonic rock is *diorite*. Granite is made up mostly of quartz and feldspar. Diorite is mostly feldspar, and has almost no quartz.

The darker plutonic rocks have pyroxene and olivine in them. *Gabbro* has some feldspar and no quartz, but much pyroxene and some olivine. Some rocks, like *serpentine*, contain mixtures of pyroxene and olivine, but no feldspar or quartz at all. The Palisades, the high cliffs that stand above the New Jersey shore of the Hudson River, are made of a fine-grained gabbro called *diabase*.

A WALL IN SOLID ROCK

Sometimes an igneous rock is found as a wall in solid rock. A different kind of rock surrounds it on

57

both sides, as shown in the drawing on page 59. This kind of wall-in-a-rock is called a *dike*. The dike tells us that a long time ago a pool of magma formed and grew deep underground. The magma pushed up against the rock layers above it and made them crack. Then magma flowed upwards into the cracks, widened them, and hardened to form the dikes.

ROCK SANDWICHES

When magma broke into a sedimentary rock, sometimes it flowed between the layers of the rock. Then when it hardened, sheets of igneous rock were sandwiched between layers of sedimentary rock. These sheets of igneous rock are known as *sills*.

A HALF-AND-HALF ROCK

Porphyry is an igneous rock in which large crystals are surrounded by a mass of tiny crystals. This combination of large and small crystals tells how the rock was formed in two steps. First a mass of magma

58

pushed its way into the rocks deep down under the ground. It cooled slowly, so some large crystals were formed. But before the magma had hardened completely, a crack opened up in the rock above the magma. Some of the magma was pushed up through

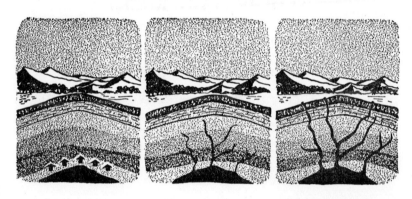

How dikes were made

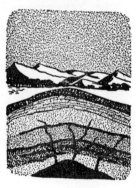

How sills were made

59

the crack and flowed out on the surface as lava. Here, as it cooled quickly, small crystals were formed around the big crystals. So porphyry is half plutonic and half volcanic rock.

SEDIMENTARY ROCKS

MAN-MADE ROCK

One of our important building materials is a man-made rock called *concrete*. We use it to make the foundations of buildings. We also use it to build roads, city pavements, bridges, and dams.

We make concrete at the place where it will be used. You can see how this is done by watching masons "pouring" the foundation of a house. The raw materials they use are gravel, sand, cement, and water. They dump these into the metal barrel of a concrete-mixer. While a gasoline engine turns the barrel, the gravel, sand, cement, and water are thoroughly mixed. Then the mixture is poured into a mold. In the mixture, each pebble of the gravel and each grain of sand are surrounded by the wet cement. As the cement dries, it hardens. The hardening cement grips every pebble and grain of sand and binds it to its neighbors. In a few days the mixture "sets" and becomes solid as a rock.

NATURE'S CONCRETE

There is a natural rock that is made in the same way. Without the help of a mason, without metal barrels or gasoline engines, nature brings together gravel and sand, and binds them together with a cement. The natural force that does all the work is water. Water picks up stones and sand as it washes over the soil and pours into the streams. Water drops them again, to form layers of gravel and sand. The water also brings the cement that binds the sand and gravel together. As the water washes over rocks and through the soil, it dissolves calcite and other minerals. Later, when the water trickles through layers of gravel and sand, some of the calcite comes out of the water and forms a coat around each pebble and grain of sand. As more calcite comes out of the water, the coats become thicker, until they fill all the spaces between the pebbles and grains of sand. The calcite grips the pebbles and sand and binds them together to form a rock. A rock formed in this way is called *conglomerate* if the gravel in it is made of smooth pebbles. If the gravel consist of rough stones, the rock is called *breccia*.

Conglomerate and breccia are formed in stream beds, where gravel and sand are dropped by flowing water. But sometimes we find conglomerate and breccia where there is no stream. They may be deep under the ground, covered by other rocks. Then we know that there must have been a stream there a long time ago when the conglomerate or breccia were formed. We know, too, that the stream flowed rapidly, because only swiftly moving water can carry stones. But then there must have been hills or moun-

62

tains near by, because water flows swiftly only when slopes are steep. Wherever we find conglomerate and breccia, they tell this story of mountains and swift streams of the past.

CEMENTED SAND

After a stream has dropped its load of gravel, it may still move fast enough to carry sand and mud. Later, when it slows down some more, it drops the sand while holding on to the mud. Piles of sand are built up along the banks of streams and at the mouths of rivers. In the ocean, waves and currents push the sand around on the floor of the sea and lift it up to the beaches. On the beaches the wind joins in the work of carrying the sand, blowing it into big piles called *dunes*.

On the beaches, sea shells are scattered in the sand. They are pounded and smashed by the waves, and then ground into tiny pieces by the shifting sand. The shell fragments are mixed with the quartz grains

63

that make up most of the sand lying on the beach.

At the bottom of a pile of sand the grains are packed tight. They are not free to move. Water trickles through and coats them with calcite. The calcite serves as a cement that binds the grains of sand together. The sand pile becomes a rock known as *sandstone*. When you look at sandstone under a microscope you can see the grains of sand and the shell fragments held together by the calcite cement. In some sandstone the grains of sand are large and easy to see. In others the grains are very fine. The grains of sand in sandstone are tougher than the calcite cement that holds them together. So, when you break a piece of sandstone, it usually breaks around the grains instead of across them.

HARDENED MUD

Most of the load that rivers carry is mud. They drop some of the mud on the plains along their banks when they overflow. They drop most of it on

64

the bottom of the sea. Some streams flow into lakes and leave their burden of mud there. The mud piles up, layer on layer. The lower layers are pressed and cemented to form *shale*.

When water flows across a mud floor, it leaves its footprints in the form of flow lines in the mud. These flow lines may remain even after more mud is piled over them, and the mud hardens into shale. When you break a piece of shale you will often find in it these footprints of the water that built the rock.

In the sea, dead animals and plants fall to the sea floor and lie in the mud. The soft parts of the animals and plants rot. The hard parts, like shells and skeletons, may be ground up. But some are covered by the mud and preserved in the shale that is formed. Later the sea may dry out, or the sea floor may be lifted out of the sea, leaving the shale high and dry. But the shells are still there, to help tell the story of shale, the story of rock formed from mud under water.

65

Shale is made up mostly of clay. It usually also has some mica and quartz in it, as well as other minerals. Some shales are black because they have large amounts of carbon left by rotted plants and animals.

ROCK MADE FROM SHELLS

While flowing water *pushes* and *carries* mud, sand, and gravel, it also *dissolves* salts that are in the rocks and soil. Then the rivers carry these salts with them to the sea. One of the salts brought to the sea is the mineral calcite. Animals living in the sea take the calcite out of the water to build their shells out of it. Some of these shells are big, like the shells of oysters and clams. Others are so small you have to use a microscope to see them. When the animals die, the shells pile up on the floor of the sea. In this way, as thousands of years go by, the animals build up layers of calcite mud on the sea floor.

Calcite also falls out of the water in the form of

crystals. The crystals pile up with the shells. Then the whole mass is pressed and cemented to form a rock called *limestone*. Most limestone in the ground tells a story of old seas that have disappeared. The fa-

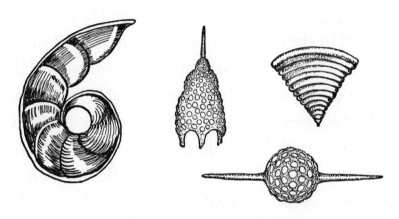

Shells of microscopic animals that help
to form limestone

mous white cliffs of Dover, England, are made of limestone.

Some limestone is formed when calcite crystals fall out of *hot springs* that bubble out of the ground.

67

There are hot-spring deposits in Yellowstone National Park.

LIMESTONE CAVES

Wherever there is limestone in the ground you may expect to find underground caves. The caves are formed by the water that soaks into the ground when it rains. The water contains some carbonic acid, which can dissolve calcite, the mineral in limestone. First the water seeps into cracks in the limestone. As the limestone dissolves, the cracks grow wider. More water flows in and dissolves more of the rock. Over the years, as the water eats its way through the rock, cracks grow slowly into tunnels, and tunnels grow into caves. In some limestone regions, rain water now flows so rapidly into cracks and caves in the ground that there are no streams on the surface. The streams flow underground instead. This is true of the land near the famous Mammoth Cave in Kentucky. The cave is a complicated network of underground passages. About one hundred and fifty miles of these passages have been explored. Echo River, located about one thousand feet under the ground, is three quarters of a mile long.

DRIPSTONE

A limestone cave is damp. Water trickles along the roof of the cave. Where drops of water cling to the limestone, some of the water evaporates. When the water evaporates, the calcite in it is left as a thin layer attached to the roof. When more water evaporates, it adds another layer of calcite. Gradually, a bump of calcite appears on the roof of the cave. As more water trickles over it, it grows downward like an icicle. This pointed stone that grows down from the roof of the cave is called a *dripstone*, because it was built up by the water dripping from the roof.

Where the water drips to the floor of the cave, another dripstone begins to grow upwards from the floor. After it has grown high enough, it may join

69

the dripstone hanging from the roof. The dripstones in caves form many interesting shapes. Some look like castles. Some look like organ pipes. There are weird shapes, too, unlike anything else we know. A trip through an underground limestone cave is like a journey through a fairyland.

ROCKS BUILT BY ANIMALS

One of the most interesting sedimentary rocks is *coral*. It is made of calcite, so it is a kind of limestone. Like other limestones, it is formed in water. But it doesn't merely pile up from crystals and shells that settle out of the water. It is *built* by tiny animals. A coral reef is an underwater apartment house built by the jellylike animals that live in it.

Coral animals live only in shallow warm water. They build the reef that they live in out of calcite that they get from the sea water. The animals do not leave the reef. The reef is like a hard sponge. Water flows through the holes in it, bringing the coral ani-

70

mals their food. As the animals grow and multiply, new layers are built on the reef.

When a reef is first built along the shores of an island, it is a *fringing reef*. Some were turned into *barrier reefs* and *atoll reefs* when the islands they surrounded sank into the sea. The settling land carried the coral down into deeper water. But the coral animals cannot live at a depth below 150 feet. They had to build the reefs higher to stay nearer the surface, where they could live. A built-up reef formed a wall or barrier, separated by a lagoon from the island it surrounded. If the island disappeared completely beneath the water of the lagoon, the barrier reef became an atoll reef.

There are places where coral is found on dry land, far from the warm seas where the coral animal lives. This shows that the land must have been under water, long ago, when the coral was built. Coral found in west Texas is one sign that parts of the United States were once covered by warm, shallow seas.

EVOLUTION OF AN ATOLL
[*Above*] Fringing reef   [*Below*] Barrier reef   [*Opposite*] Atoll

Sometimes limestone is changed by chemical action into another kind of rock. Limestone is made of calcite. One of the chemicals in calcite is *calcium*. The sea water that surrounds the limestone contains *magnesium*. As the water soaks through the limestone, the calcium and magnesium may change places. The calcium returns to the sea water, and the magnesium takes its place in the rock. When this

73

happens, the limestone is changed into *dolomite*. Although the chemical nature of the rock is changed, its shape remains the same. The lower levels of some coral reefs have dolomite in them.

CHERT AND FLINT

While most sea shells are made of calcite, some, formed by tiny animals and plants, are made of quartz. These quartz shells also pile up under water. At the same time, some small quartz crystals form from quartz that is dissolved in the water. They join the shells and cement them into sedimentary rock. One of these rocks is *chert*. Lumps of chert are found in some deposits of limestone or dolomite. The *flint* formerly used for making arrows and spear points is a dark-colored chert.

PETRIFIED WOOD

Thousands of years ago some trees fell and were buried under mud. In the water that seeped through

74

the mud some quartz had dissolved. As the wood slowly rotted, the chemicals that were formed changed places with the quartz. The rotted wood was carried away by the water. Tiny quartz crystals filled the spaces where the wood used to be. Finally no wood was left. But the quartz that took its place had the shape of the wood. Rock formed in this way is called *petrified wood* (wood turned into stone). While the petrified wood was being formed, the mud that surrounded it was being turned into shale. Years later, the shale became part of dry land. When the soft shale was worn away by weathering, the hard petrified wood was uncovered.

THE ROCK WE BURN

The coal we burn in our furnaces is a black rock dug up out of the ground. The miners who dig the coal sometimes find whole tree stumps in the coal. These buried trees are clues to how the coal was formed. *All coal is formed from buried plants.*

75

About three hundred million years ago, Pennsylvania, West Virginia, Ohio, and Illinois were partly covered by shallow seas. Great forests of giant ferns and cattails grew in the swamps next to these seas. Plants that died rotted in the swamp to form a thick pasty muck called *peat*. More and more plants grew and died in the swamp, building up layers of peat hundreds of feet thick. Later the sea rose over the swamp and covered it with mud and sand. The mud and sand and water, pressing down on the peat, squeezed the juices out of it and compressed it. While the mud became shale, and the sand became sandstone, the peat became coal. Every twenty feet of peat was squeezed into one foot of coal. In some places the land rose out of the sea again, and the same process was repeated. A new forest grew in a swamp. Another layer of peat was formed and buried. A second layer of coal was formed over the first one. The coal formed in this way is *bituminous coal*, also known as *soft coal*. Like shale and sandstone, it is a

76

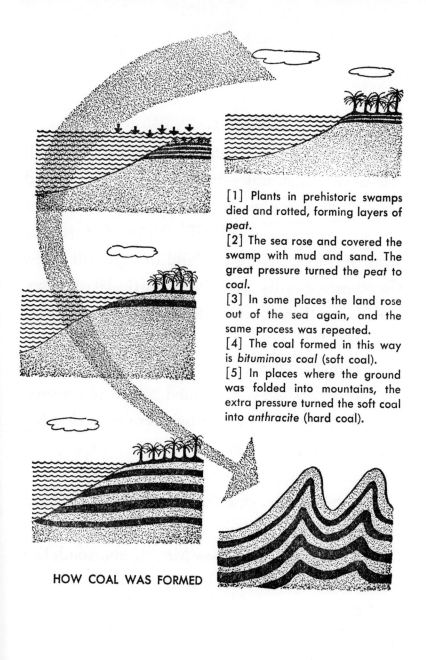

[1] Plants in prehistoric swamps died and rotted, forming layers of *peat*.

[2] The sea rose and covered the swamp with mud and sand. The great pressure turned the *peat* to *coal*.

[3] In some places the land rose out of the sea again, and the same process was repeated.

[4] The coal formed in this way is *bituminous coal* (soft coal).

[5] In places where the ground was folded into mountains, the extra pressure turned the soft coal into *anthracite* (hard coal).

HOW COAL WAS FORMED

member of the family of sedimentary rocks.

SEAS THAT DRIED UP

Large parts of the United States were once, millions of years ago, under shallow seas. When the land rose up out of the water, most of the seas drained off into the Atlantic and Pacific Oceans. But parts of them were trapped on the land to form salt lakes. The climate was dry, so the water of the lakes evaporated faster than it was replaced by rain. The lakes dried up. The water was gone, but the salt in the water remained behind. This is how large deposits of halite or *rock salt* were formed. Layers of *gypsum*, another salt found in sea water, were formed in the same way. There are thick deposits of rock salt in New York, Michigan, Kansas, Oklahoma, and Texas. Near Detroit, Michigan, the salt bed is six hundred feet thick. There are large gypsum deposits in New York, Oklahoma, Texas, New Mexico, and South Dakota. Plaster of Paris is made from gypsum.

78

METAMORPHIC ROCKS

HOW ROCKS ARE CHANGED

If a rock is squeezed hard enough and made hot enough, it can be changed into another kind of rock. The heat and the pressure break up the minerals in the rock. The chemicals in the old minerals are rearranged to form new minerals, or new crystals of the old minerals. Hot gases and liquids that flow past the rock may join in the work of changing it. The kind of rock that results depends on what the rock was in the first place. It also depends on how hard it was squeezed, and how hot it was made.

CHANGE BY INVASION

When hot magma invades a rock, pushing its way into cracks, or spreading out between layers, it heats and squeezes the rock that it touches. This is sometimes enough to make the rock change. Steam and

79

hot water brought by the magma may also play a part in the change. So, while the magma itself becomes an igneous rock, the rock it touches may become a metamorphic rock. That's why metamorphic rocks are sometimes found next to dikes and sills. When magma invades a fine-grained rock like shale, it may change it into *hornfels*. Hornfels is very hard and fine-grained. It breaks into sharp jagged pieces.

When sandstone is changed over by heat and pressure, the old grains of sand disappear. New, tightly packed grains of quartz take their place. The new rock is called *quartzite*. It is very hard, and looks sugary. While most sandstone breaks around its grains, quartzite breaks across its grains.

When limestone or dolomite is changed by heat, pressure, and the action of hot water, they are turned into *marble*. Marble also looks sugary, but is soft compared with quartzite. Quartzite is hard enough to scratch glass. Marble is soft enough to be scratched by a copper penny. Marble often has light and dark streaks in it.

CHANGE BY FOLDING

When you push the ends of a carpet together, it buckles and forms folds. Some layers of rock have been folded in this way. In the lower layers the heat

and pressure were enough to change the rock. Large masses of changed, folded rocks are found in mountain ranges.

When shale is changed by heat and pressure, the clay in it is turned into mica, and the shale may be turned into *slate*. Slate is fine-grained, and splits into broad sheets with dull surfaces. Still greater pressure and heat can turn shale and some other rocks into *mica schist*. Mica schist is made up of tightly packed small wavy flakes of mica and quartz. The most common rock on the island of Manhattan in New York is a dark-gray mica schist. The flakes of mica in it can be seen distinctly.

Granite, shale, mica schist, and some other rocks can be changed over to form another metamorphic rock called *gneiss*. Gneiss, like granite, has large crystals in it, but they are arranged in bands. The bands make it look like a layer cake with filling. Gneisses contain much feldspar, together with quartz, mica, and some other minerals.

82

When the rocks in the Appalachian Mountains were folded, the coal in the ground got the same heat and pressure treatment the other rocks received.

Metamorphic rocks were formed by heat (from magma) and pressure.

Mountains were formed by folding.

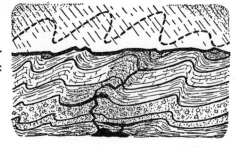

Weathering wore down outer layers. Now metamorphic rocks are on the surface.

83

When the soft coal was squeezed, it was turned into *anthracite,* or *hard coal.*

WHERE THE INSIDE IS OUTSIDE

Geologists have proved that large amounts of metamorphic rocks are formed only at great depths under the ground, where the pressure and temperature are very high. This is true especially of flaky rocks like schist, sheet-like rocks like slate, and banded rocks like gneiss. They were formed inside the earth, with thousands of feet of other rocks pressing down on them. But now we find rocks like these on the outside, on the surface of the earth. This means that the rocks that used to be above them were worn away. They were broken up by weathering and carried away by rain water.

The Not-So-Everlasting Rocks

☞ **A** BIG rock looks as though it will last forever. Animals live and die, but the rock stays on and on. Trees shed their leaves each fall, but the rock looks the same, summer and winter. While all other things move, or grow, or change, the rock doesn't seem to change at all.

But actually rocks *do* change, and they do not last forever. The stories in the rocks are all stories of action, movement, and change. Soil tells the story of how rocks break up and rot. Shale and sandstone tell of soil carried away by rivers. Sedimentary rocks that are high and dry tell of land raised out of the sea.

Slate and schist tell of rocks that were pushed and folded. Dikes and sills tell of magma that rose from inside the earth. Rocks, like everything else in the world, have a true history, with a beginning and an end. They go through many changes. Some changes are slow, like the weathering of granite. Others are fast, like earthquakes and the eruption of volcanoes.

THE EARTH BLOWS ITS TOP

Volcanoes are scenes of violent action in the rocks. The force behind most of the action is the force of *steam*. Water is mixed with the magma underground. The heat of the magma turns the water into steam. In some volcanoes the steam escapes in a steady stream, or in short spurts, through cracks or fissures. But in others the steam is trapped. Old cracks in the volcano were sealed when lava hardened in them. The steam is held down by the weight of the rock that is over it. Meanwhile, as more steam is formed, the pressure of the steam increases. Finally the steam pushes

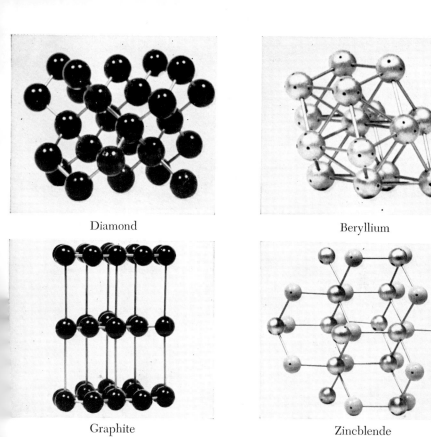

Diamond

Beryllium

Graphite

Zincblende

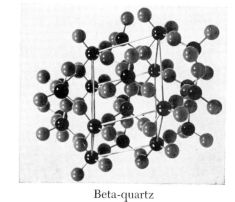

Pyrites

Beta-quartz

MODELS OF CRYSTAL STRUCTURE

Salt Crystal

Gypsum

Feldspar

Mica

Iceland spar

Quartz

MINERALS

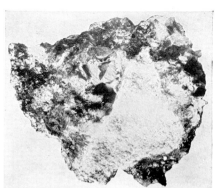

Chalcopyrite (copper ore)

Sphalerite (zinc ore)

Galena (lead ore)

Magnetite (iron ore)

Pebbles of hematite (iron ore)

Metal Ores

Slate

Pumice

Basalt

Agate

Flint

Gneiss

Rocks [1]

Marble

Schist

Gabbro

Sandstone

Granite

Porphyry

Rocks [2]

A copper ore mine in Bingham Canyon

Iron ore mine in Hibbing, Minn.

OPEN PIT MINES

Pulsator table for separating diamonds from crushed ore

Prospector panning gravel for diamonds

Diamond Mining in South Africa

Dripstones in Luray Caverns

Calcite terraces from Hot Springs in Yellowstone National Park

CALCITE DEPOSITS FROM GROUND WATER

Petrified wood

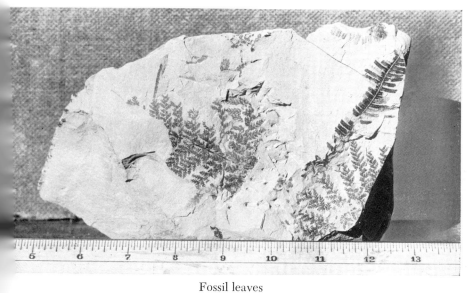

Fossil leaves

EVIDENCE OF PAST LIFE

Blocks of granite leaving the quarry

A granite quarry in Vermont

GRANITE

New volcano born in 1943 near Parícutin, Mexico

Rocks hardened from a river of lava. Craters of the Moon National Monument

Volcanoes

Boulders left behind by the glaciers of the last Ice Age

GLACIERS [1]

Glacial boulder in Yellowstone National Park

Potholes on top of Sentinel Dome in Yosemite National Park

GLACIERS [2]

A press that makes artificial diamonds. One of the diamonds is shown in the inset

Artificial Diamonds

A Diamond Cutter at Work in Johannesburg, South Africa

Carnotite

Autunite

Pitchblende

Beryl

Torbernite

Monazite

MINERALS FOR ATOMIC ENERGY

up hard enough to move the rock. A great explosion takes place as the volcano "erupts." The escaping steam blows lava and broken rock into the air. Fragments of rock and hardening lava shower down on the ground. They pile up in a *cinder cone* around the hole from which they were blown. The next time the volcano erupts, the cone is built higher. After many eruptions, the volcano becomes a cone-shaped mountain.

AN ISLAND DIES

The island of Krakatau, located between Java and Sumatra, rose 2,600 feet out of the sea. It was a cinder cone built up a long time ago by eruptions of a volcano. In 1883 the volcano erupted once more. A great explosion of steam shattered the island. It blew about a cubic mile of broken rock into the air. A cloud of steam and flying rock rose seventeen miles above the ground. Millions of tons of rock and dust rained down over the surrounding sea. The winds carried dust from the explosion all around the world. Krakatau was gone. In its place was a great hole, one thousand feet deep under the sea.

The explosion that wiped out Krakatau sent waves one hundred feet high racing across the sea. The waves killed thousands of people when they struck the coasts of Java and Sumatra.

AN ISLAND IS BORN

The eruption of volcanoes has created new islands where none existed before. Lava, flowing out of cracks in the sea floor, piled up layer on layer, until it was high enough to rise out of the sea. A new island was formed in this way, about two hundred miles south of Tokyo, Japan, in February 1953. It rose out of reefs that had been thrown up half a year before.

One new island, called Falcon Island, in the South Seas, has had its ups and downs over the years. It was sighted as a low reef from a British warship in 1865. In 1894 it rose 50 feet out of the water. In the next four years it took such a beating from the waves that it was worn down to a shoal. By 1928 it was up again to a new height of 600 feet above sea level. In 1938 it was down again to 30 feet. In 1953 it was completely under water, 75 feet below the surface.

VOLCANO IN A CORNFIELD

A new volcano was born in Mexico on February 5, 1943. It poked its head out of the ground in a peaceful cornfield three miles from the village of Parícutin. Steam and lava poured out of its mouth. The mouth widened into a great crater, and cinders piled up around it to build a great cone. Rivers of lava flowed from the crater. They spread over near-by fields and forced the villagers of Parícutin to flee. The baby volcano has grown to a height of 1,500 feet.

THE GROUND HEAVES

The violence of volcanoes is matched by the violence of earthquakes. Earthquakes take place along

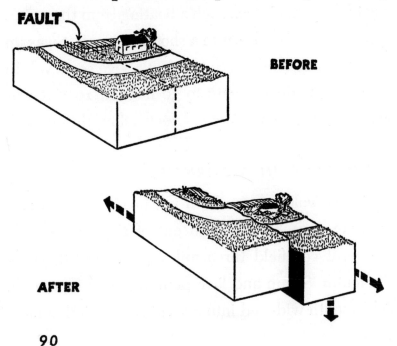

FAULT

BEFORE

AFTER

great cracks in the ground called *faults*. The ground heaves as the land masses on both sides of the fault suddenly slide along each other. In one earthquake in Japan, the ground on one side of the fault rose to form a cliff 18 feet high. At the same time it slid sideways 12 feet.

The earthquake that wrecked the city of San Francisco in 1906 took place along the San Andreas Rift. The Rift is a great crack in the ground that cuts

91

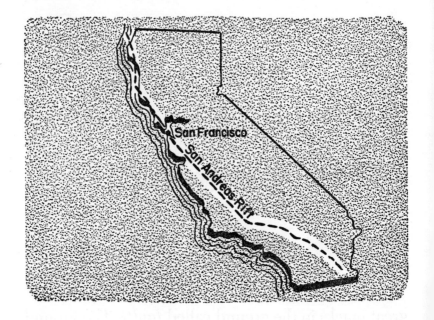

through the whole length of California. It follows the coast in the northern part of the state, until it reaches San Francisco. There it turns inland and continues south into the Colorado Desert. In the 1906 earthquake, the ground was ripped open along the Rift. The land on the west side of the Rift moved north, in some places as far as 21 feet.

In 1899 an earthquake in Alaska raised a large part

92

of the shore out of the sea. Part of the sea floor became dry land, and the old beach was lifted to a height of 47 feet.

When the land moves sideways along a fault, rocks that were next to each other on opposite sides of the fault are separated. By measuring how far they are separated, we can tell how far the ground slid along the fault. In Scotland, rocks that used to be next to one another along the Great Glen Fault are now 65 miles apart. A separation this great may be the result of many earthquakes in the past, or of a long period of gradual sliding along the fault.

RISING SHORES

It doesn't always take a volcano or an earthquake to raise land out of the sea. In some parts of the world the land is rising hour by hour, and day by day. The rise is slow but steady. The shores of Sweden and Finland are rising about three feet every hundred years. Meanwhile some land is sinking. South-

93

ern Denmark is settling into the sea at the rate of two feet every century.

In Naples, Italy, there is proof that the shore sank over 18 feet into the sea, and then rose again, all during the last two thousand years. The proof is in the ruins of an old temple built by the ancient Romans. All that remains of the temple are several stone columns about 50 feet high. Up to a height of 18 feet above the floor, each column is rough and full of small holes. Above this height the columns are smooth. The holes in the columns tell the story of how the land sank and then rose again. The temple was built on dry land. When the land sank into the sea, the water flooded the shore, and reached 18 feet above the floor of the temple. Clams that lived in the water bored holes in the columns of the temple. Then the land rose out of the sea again. Now the temple is high and dry once more, but the holes in the bottom of the columns tell about the centuries they spent under water.

FLOATING ROCKS

A lump of modeling clay is solid. But when you squeeze it, it flows like a liquid. A rock that is squeezed hard enough will flow, too. This actually happens to the rocks that are deep under the ground. They are squeezed very hard by the rocks that press down on them from above. The pressure turns the underground rocks into a vast slow-moving ocean. The crust of the earth is made up of giant rafts of rock floating on this ocean of slowly flowing rock. A fault in the crust is where one raft lies next to another.

When you step onto a raft that is floating on water, it becomes heavier and sinks more deeply into the water. When you get off the raft, you remove the extra load, and the raft rises higher in the water. This is a clue to the reason why the land rises or sinks. It sinks where the load on it is increased. It rises when part of the load on it is removed.

DRIFTING LAND

There are currents in the ocean of slowly flowing rock that is deep under the ground. The rock rafts floating on this ocean drift with the currents. But two rafts that lie next to each other may be drifting in opposite directions. If they are pressed together tightly along the fault that separates them, they may not slide along the fault at first. They rub against each other, and stick. But as the tugging of the underground currents continues, the force trying to pull the rafts apart grows stronger and stronger. Finally this force becomes stronger than the force that hold the rafts together at the fault. They begin to slide in one sudden movement. The earth heaves, as another earthquake rocks the land.

RIVERS OF ICE

The snow that piles up on the ground in the wintertime usually melts and runs off in the springtime. But at the top of a high mountain the air is so cold even in the spring and summer that the snow doesn't melt completely. Snow stays on the ground there all year round. When more snow is added year after year, the snowflakes are pressed together to form little balls of ice. After a while the ice is piled so high it can't stand up under its own weight. The ice begins to flow. A slow-moving river of ice, called a *glacier,* descends from the mountaintop into the valleys below. At lower altitudes, where the air is warmer, the ice begins to melt. There is a large glacier on Mount Rainier in the state of Washington.

Glaciers can grow and then shrink again. After a series of cold winters with heavy snowfalls, a glacier grows, and spreads out over more land. In warm years it retreats as the ice along its edges melts.

ICE SHEETS OVER CONTINENTS

The largest glaciers are found near the north and south poles. They are giant sheets of ice covering whole continents. All of Greenland, with an area of over 600,000 square miles, is under ice. The ice sheet on the continent of Antarctica covers an area of 5,000,000 square miles.

About one million years ago, the climate of the earth was colder. The polar ice sheets grew and spread out, and the glaciers on the mountains came down to the plains. In the Northern Hemisphere the ice invaded large areas of Asia, Europe, and North America, and stayed during an *age of ice*. Then the climate became warmer, and the ice sheet retreated as it melted. The ice sheet came down again during three more ice ages after that. The last ice age ended about ten thousand years ago.

CALLING CARD OF A GLACIER

We can tell how far south the ice came during the ice ages, because it left its calling card. It also left easily recognized footprints and fingerprints on the land.

98

When a glacier moves along the ground, it is like a giant chisel. It scrapes the soil off the ground and chips off pieces of rock. On its back it carries rocks that fall on it from neighboring cliffs. It brings its load of soil and rock with it when it spreads out. Then it drops the load when the ice melts. The ice sheet that came south during the ice ages carried some rocks hundreds of miles before dropping them. The rocks were rounded and polished by the rubbing they got during their long journey. They were often left over land made of a different kind of rock, so they are easily recognized as intruders. They are the calling cards of the glacier, left as reminders of its presence.

When a glacier pushed its way between hills, it gouged out a U-shaped path that is different from the V-shaped valleys of streams and rivers. The U-shaped valleys are the footprints of the glacier.

Under the glacier were some of the boulders that it picked up on the way. As the glacier pushed its way along, these boulders made long scratches on the bedrock they passed over. These scratches or *striations* are the fingerprints of the glacier.

As the ice melted, streams of water began to flow under the ice, carrying some rocks with them. They tumbled over cliffs in waterfalls under the ice. At the base of these cliffs, the churning water and rocks ground out big *potholes* in the bedrock. After the glacier retreated, the streams and falls disappeared, but the potholes remained, like great thumbprints, to remind us that the glacier had been there.

TRAIL TO TREASURE

In Finland, a country in northern Europe, there are many scattered rocks that are different from the local rocks they rest on. Some of them were found to contain large amounts of nickel. This meant that somewhere in the north there was a valuable deposit of nickel ore. When the ice sheet passed over this deposit during the ice age, it picked up pieces,

[*Above*] V-shaped valley of streams and rivers.

[*Below*] U-shaped valley gouged out by a glacier.

and then dropped them again on its way south. The pieces that it dropped formed a trail that ran south from the deposit. Realizing this, prospectors followed the rock trail back north and discovered the great nickel mines of Petsamo.

TWO DAMS ACROSS THE COLUMBIA RIVER

When the last ice sheet came down across Canada about twenty thousand years ago, it put out a tongue across the Columbia River in the state of Washington. The ice formed a huge dam that prevented the water from following its usual course. The river, swollen with water that flowed out of the ice sheet, overflowed across the Columbia Plateau. The sand and rock carried by the water made it a good cutting tool. The river ground out several new channels for itself in the basalt rock of the plateau. The largest of these, known as the Grand Coulee, is a canyon from 500 to 1,000 feet deep. Halfway down the Grand Coulee the river fell over a waterfall 400 feet high and nearly three miles wide. When the ice sheet melted, the river returned to its old channel, leaving the Grand Coulee dry.

Now there is another dam across the Columbia River, where the old ice dam used to be. This one, built by men, was completed in 1942. The flow of water over the dam turns turbines to make electric power. Some of this power will be used to pump water through the Grand Coulee to irrigate land that is too dry.

The glacier pushed many rivers out of their old beds and forced them to cut new channels. While the Columbia River returned to its old bed when the ice melted, some rivers stayed in their new beds.

MELT-WATER LAKES

The ice sheets that came down into the United States from Canada dug out big basins between the two countries. When the ice melted, the melt-water flowed into these basins to form huge fresh-water lakes. As the ice advanced and retreated during the four ice ages, these ancient lakes changed their shapes many times. Some of them became the chain of Great Lakes that stretches from Minnesota to New York. The ancient lakes were larger than the Great Lakes of today. The old shore lines remain, high up on the land, showing us how far the lakes reached in the past.

One of the lakes of melt-water was Lake Bonneville, covering a large part of what is now the state of Utah. Thousands of years of dry climate caused most of this lake to evaporate. While the water of the lake evaporated, the salt in it remained behind. So the shrinking lake became saltier and saltier. What is left of it is the Great Salt Lake of Utah. The shore line of old Lake Bonneville can still be seen on the slopes of the Wasatch Mountains, 1,000 feet above the surface of Great Salt Lake.

ICE A MILE HIGH

Where the ice sheet rubbed against a mountain we can see how high the ice reached. The ice that covered New England was more than 4,000 feet thick. Farther north the ice must have been thicker. The weight of this ice put a great load on the land, and forced it to sink. When the ice melted, the load was removed, and the land rose again. As the land rose north of the Great Lakes, the old shore lines of the ancient lakes were tilted. These tilted beaches help to show how much the land has risen since the end of the ice age.

The great load of ice that pressed down on countries in the far north made them sink very deep. When the ice melted, they began to rise again. But they haven't reached their old levels yet. That's why Sweden and Finland are still rising out of the sea, at a rate of three feet every hundred years.

105

CONTINENTS AND OCEANS

Every continent is a large raft of rock floating on the flowing rock beneath it. The floor under every ocean is also a raft of rock floating on the same mass of flowing underground rock. But the continents are floating higher than the floor of the oceans. This shows that the rock of the ocean floor is heavier than the rock of the continents. The ocean floor is made up mostly of basalt. The continents are made up mostly of granite, resting on a layer of basalt. When the crust of the earth was formed billions of years ago, it was made up mainly of these two types of rock, granite and basalt. The basalt formed a complete sphere around the earth, like the skin of an orange. The granite, being lighter in weight than the basalt, floated on top of it. Large chunks of floating granite made up the continents. They were separated by great basins with basalt bottoms. Then, when the first rains came pouring out of the sky, the water natu-

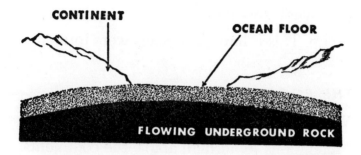

CONTINENT

OCEAN FLOOR

FLOWING UNDERGROUND ROCK

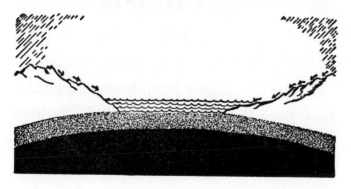

rally flowed downhill into these basins and filled them up. This is how the oceans were formed.

THE ROOTS OF MOUNTAINS

While the continents stand high above the oceans, the mountains stand high above the continents. But the mountains, too, are floating on the rock that is deep underground. The raft of rock that is under a mountain is pressed down by the great load that it carries. So, like a great floating ship, a mountain is only partly above the surface. Every mountain has a giant root that is deep under the ground.

HOW MOUNTAINS ARE BORN

The rocks in mountains have folds in them, like a carpet whose ends have been pushed together. To explain how mountains are born, geologists had to find a natural force that could fold the rocks in that way. They believe they have found this force in currents

108

in the flowing rock beneath the granite and basalt crust of the earth.

The layer of flowing rock that lies under the crust of the earth is called the *mantle*. It is almost two thousand miles thick. The mantle connects the core of the earth, which is very hot, with the crust of the earth, which is cool. The mantle transfers heat from the core to the crust. One way in which it transfers the heat is by flowing. Rock heated near the core becomes lighter and floats up toward the crust. Meanwhile cool rock near the crust sinks down to take its place. This makes the rock in the mantle flow in a circle, as shown in the diagram on page 110. There may be many such circular currents in the mantle. The diagram on page 111 shows two of these currents side by side. Near the crust, the currents move toward each other, and then flow down where they come together. They drag against the floating crust and pull it down where the currents meet. This

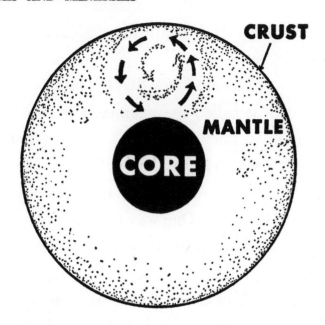

makes a dent in the surface of the earth. Rivers flow
into this dent and fill it with sediment. Gradually,
layers of sedimentary rocks are built up in this dent.
Meanwhile the underground currents keep pressing
in on these rocks and pulling them down. The rocks
are folded and crushed. As they are pulled down, the
root of the mountain is formed and grows. *A mountain has been born, but it is all underground.* The

110

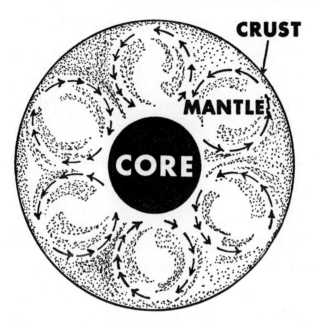

two circular currents in the mantle keep dragging it down, so it cannot float up out of the ground. This condition continues as long as there is cool rock near the crust, and hot rock in the mantle near the core.

The rocks in the root are pressed and heated deep inside the mantle. As a result they are changed into metamorphic rocks. The bottom of the root is melted to form magma. Where the magma breaks

111

into the crust, igneous rocks are formed as it cools.

As the currents keep flowing in the mantle, they bring cool rock down to the bottom of the mantle, and hot rock up to the top. This cools off the bottom of the mantle, and warms up the top near the crust. Gradually the currents slow down, and finally they stop. But when the currents stop flowing, the force that was dragging the root of the mountain down is gone. The mountain, not held down any more, begins to rise up out of the ground.

There are four stages in the history of the circular currents in the mantle. In the first stage, the currents are slowly picking up speed. This stage probably

HOW MOUNTAINS ARE BORN
[1] When the currents come together, [2] they pull down the crust and make a dent in the surface of the earth. [3] Rivers fill the dent with sediment [4] and build up layers of sedimentary rock. [5] The downward pull folds and crushes the rocks. The root of the mountain is formed. [6] Bottom of the root melts and forms magma. Some may break into the crust. [7] Bottom of mantle cools. Top of mantle, near crust, warms up. Currents slow down, then stop. [8] The mountain, no longer pulled down by currents, begins to rise above ground.

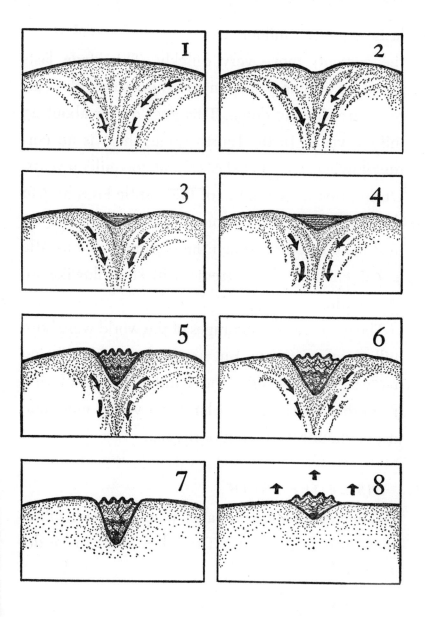

lasts about 25 million years. In the second stage, the currents move very quickly. This stage lasts about 10 million years. In the third stage, the currents are slowing down. This goes on for about 25 million years. In the fourth stage, there is no current flowing. This stage lasts about 500 million years. During this stage the top of the mantle loses heat to the crust, while the bottom of the mantle picks up heat from the core. When the bottom of the mantle is hot enough, the currents will start flowing all over again.

The great mountain ranges of the world were born millions of years ago. But new mountains are being made before our eyes, in the islands of the East Indies in southeast Asia. Each island is a young mountain just beginning to rise out of the sea.

INSIDE THE EARTH

When an earthquake takes place, it sends vibrations through the earth. The vibrations can be detected, even at places thousands of miles from the earthquake, on an instrument called the *seismo-graph*. The speed of the vibrations gives us clues to the weight and stiffness of the material inside the earth. We get more clues from the way the vibrations bounce and turn as they travel through the earth. By putting all these clues together with other known facts, geologists have formed a picture of the inside of the earth.

The earth is a great ball. Its center is about 4,000 miles under the surface. It is made up of three main parts, all of which have already been mentioned. At the surface is the *crust*. Under the oceans the crust is nearly all basalt. In the continents, there is granite resting on the basalt, and sedimentary rock lying on the granite. The crust of the earth is only about 25 miles thick.

Beneath the crust is the *mantle*, extending almost 2,000 miles toward the center of the earth. It is solid rock, but it can flow slowly. Because it flows, it

115

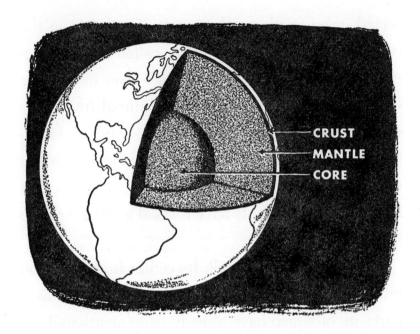

is like a great ocean of rock on which the crust floats. The mantle is probably made of *peridotite*, an igneous rock that is heavier than basalt, and has very large amounts of olivine in it.

At the center is the *core*, made up of iron and nickel. The core itself is divided into two parts. The outer part is liquid; the inner part is probably solid.

HOW IT ALL BEGAN

There are many different theories of how the earth was formed. For a while scientists thought it was formed from a mass of hot gas torn out of the sun by a passing star. The mass of gas, they said, broke up into several pieces, and each one formed a planet. According to this theory, the gas that became the earth cooled slowly. As it cooled, it collapsed into a liquid ball. Then, when it cooled some more, it became solid.

Today most scientists support a different theory. They believe that the sun and the planets were formed at the same time from whirling clouds of dust and gas. The dust and gas particles attracted each other. The pieces of dust came together to form larger and larger flakes. The flakes stuck together to form lumps. Small lumps fell into larger lumps, until, finally, several large balls were formed. Each ball kept growing as more lumps fell into it. As it grew, its own weight pressed in on its center and made it warm. The largest ball was squeezed more than the rest. It became so hot, it was turned into a glowing gas. This was the sun. The earth was formed from one of the smaller balls. It became hot enough to melt, but not hot enough to be a glowing gas. The new theory agrees with the old theory that the earth was a very hot ball of melted rock before it became solid.

The earth started out as a mixture of many chemicals. Some of them combined by chemical action. Then the combinations were partly separated by their weights. The heaviest ones sank to the center. The lightest ones floated up to the surface. This is how the core, the mantle, and the crust began to take shape. The crust is about three times as heavy as water. The mantle is from four to six times as heavy as water. The core is from ten to seventeen times as heavy as water.

THE GAS AROUND THE EARTH

While the earth was still very hot, it was surrounded by an atmosphere of poison gases. But the heat made the gas particles jump around so fast that they escaped from the earth. The first atmosphere vanished, and a new one took its place. The new atmosphere was formed from gas that bubbled out of the melted rock at the surface of the earth. Like the gas that comes out of volcanoes today, seven tenths of it was steam, and the rest was mostly carbon dioxide and nitrogen.

THE CRUST HARDENS

Meanwhile the earth cooled. As it cooled, the melted rock on the surface hardened to form the first igneous rocks in the crust. The bottom of the crust was a shell of basalt. Large rafts of granite floated on this basalt. These rafts later became the continents. Between them were big basins with basalt floors.

THE FIRST RAINS

As the earth cooled some more, the steam in the atmosphere condensed into drops of hot water. Hot rain began to fall out of the sky. The water ran

down from high places to low places on the crust. It poured into the basins and began to fill them up. The rains continued for centuries, and the oceans were born. The first rains took most of the water out of the atmosphere. What was left was three-fourths

120

carbon dioxide, mixed with some water vapor and nitrogen.

After the oceans were formed, they supplied the water for future rains. Water evaporated from the oceans. It rose into the air as vapor, and fell again as rain. Water that fell on the land flowed into the rivers, which carried the water back to the sea.

WEARING DOWN THE ROCKS

Water is the enemy of rock. As soon as the first rains fell, water began attacking the continents. Weathering crumbled the rocks to form clay, sand, and gravel. Then flowing water carried them down to

121

the sea. Mountains were worn down, and low places were filled in. The continents were ground down to sea level, and the sea invaded the land.

NEW ROCKS FROM OLD

Water is also a mother of rock. In the shallow seas that flooded the continents, sediments piled up over the floor. They were pressed down and hardened to form the first sedimentary rocks. While water wore down the rocks in some places, it built up new rocks in others.

THE LAND GETS A BOOST

By carrying rocks from one place to another, flowing water disturbed the balance of the floating rafts of rock. Where the load was increased, the ground began to sink. Where the load was removed, the ground rose. Meanwhile, the forces that build mountains were busy in the mantle, under the crust. The roots of mountains grew, and then the mountains

122

lifted their heads out of the plains and the shallow seas. The continents were raised out of the water again, and the newly formed sedimentary rocks became dry land.

REPEAT PERFORMANCE

But as soon as the continents were high again, the rains began wearing them down once more. The upper layers of sedimentary rock were crumbled and carried away. Mountains were leveled, and metamorphic rock that was deep inside them was uncovered. The sea invaded the land again, and new sedimentary rocks were formed over what was left of the old. The action was repeated, as in a movie that is shown over and over again. Through millions of years the land rose and was worn down again many times.

THE SALT IN THE SEA

The rains that fell on the land washed salt out of the rocks and carried the salt down to the sea.

When water evaporated from the sea, it left the salt behind. The water vapor became rain again, washed more salt out of the rocks, and carried it down to the sea. Each year the rivers brought a new load of salt, and the sea became saltier and saltier.

THE SALT CLOCK

Year after year the amount of salt in the sea increases. This suggested to one scientist that he might use the salt in the sea as a clock. He measured how much salt the rivers bring down to the sea each year. Then he figured out how many years it must have taken, at this rate, to make the sea as salty as it is now. His figures showed that the oceans are at least 100 million years old. Actually they must be much older. There were long periods in the past when the continents were low, or even partly covered by water. During those periods the rivers carried salt into the sea more slowly than they do now. With less salt brought down during some years, more years were needed to make the sea as salty as it is.

THE AGE OF THE EARTH

The salt clock shows that the age of the earth has to be reckoned in hundreds of millions of years. But it doesn't tell us how many hundreds of millions it is. We get a better idea of the age of the earth from another of nature's clocks, the *uranium clock*.

There is uranium in the rocks of the earth's crust. Uranium atoms *decay* or break up into smaller atoms. The breakup takes place in a series of steps. In the last step, what used to be a uranium atom ends up as an atom of lead. The atoms don't all break up at once. First one decays, then others follow. As the years go by, a rock that contains uranium has less and less uranium in it, and more and more lead. By comparing the amount of lead with the amount of uranium, scientists can tell how old the rock must be. In this way they found out that some rocks in the Black Hills of South Dakota are at least 1½ billion years old. These are the oldest rocks found in the ground in the United States.

There are older rocks, called *meteorites,* that fall from the sky. They crash in on the earth from outer space, moving at great speeds. When they enter the earth's atmosphere, the rubbing they get as they move through the air makes them hot enough to burn and glow. At night they are seen as "shooting stars" streaking across the sky. Most of them burn up completely in the air. A few of the largest ones reach the ground. The amount of uranium and lead found in some meteorites shows that they are about 4½ billion years old. The meteorites probably were formed in space at the same time that the earth first took shape from dust and gas. If so, the earth, too, is about 4½ billion years old.

LIFE BEGINS AND CHANGES

The ocean basins were giant mixing-bowls. The water that poured into them carried many chemicals.

Some were washed out of the air. Others were picked up from the rocks. In the warm water of the sea the chemicals mixed and combined. Complicated chemicals, made up of many ingredients, appeared here and there. Some broke up again; others grew. Then, perhaps two billion years ago, a new and very special combination appeared. It was *protoplasm,* a chemical jelly that was *alive.*

The first living things were probably very tiny, like the ones we can see today under a microscope. They spread to all the seas. They grew, and they began to change. One family of living things contained a green chemical called *chlorophyll.* With the help of this chemical, they made their own food out of water and carbon dioxide. This was the family of *plants.* Another family of living things, the *animals,* had no chlorophyll. They could not make their own food. They got their food by eating plants or other animals. From the sea, plants and animals later spread to the land.

Many types of animals developed. Old types died out and new types took their place. The remains of some of those which died out have been preserved as fossils in sedimentary rocks. The fossils give us a picture of how living things developed and changed. They also help us find out the ages of sedimentary rocks. Five hundred million years ago the seas were full of animals without backbones. Three hundred and twenty million years ago the age of fishes began. Two hundred and seventy million years ago the animals began to invade the land. The first to try life outside the water were the amphibians. They lived part of the time in water and part of the time on land, the way frogs do today. One hundred and eighty-five million years ago, their descendants, the reptiles, became lords of the swampy continents. Sixty million years ago, the largest reptiles, the dinosaurs, were dying out. A new family of animals, the mammals, took over. One million years ago, during the time when the ice sheets spread from the poles, man's ancestors first appeared.

NEW AIR AND NEW ROCKS

The growth of living things changed the face of the earth. It gave the earth a new atmosphere, and produced new rocks.

The atmosphere that remained after the first rains fell was three-fourths carbon dioxide, mixed with some water vapor and nitrogen. When plants developed and spread, they began to use up the carbon dioxide to make their food. At the same time they released oxygen into the air. After millions of years the air changed into a new kind of mixture. With oxygen in the air, it became possible for animals to live out of water. Today the air is about four-fifths nitrogen and one-fifth oxygen, mixed with small amounts of other gases.

As the carbon dioxide was withdrawn from the air,

129

some of it was built into the living bodies of plants and animals. Large amounts of it, too, became part of the shells worn by animals in the sea. The bodies of some plants and the shells of some animals helped to make new kinds of rock. Buried plants became coal, and piled-up layers of sea shells became limestone and dolomite.

Buried Treasure

☞ THERE are many exciting stories about hunts for treasure buried in the ground by pirates. The treasure-hunters in these stories look forward to great rewards, because the pirates had packed a great amount of treasure into a small space. The pirates were "collectors." They roamed the seas to find ships they could attack. Then they "collected" gold, silver, and precious jewels from their victims. In the typical story, they lock the treasure in a big trunk and bury it on a beach. They are always thoughtful enough to leave a map or a message in code to guide the lucky hunters. Most of these treasure-hunts never really happened. The stories about them are only make-believe, and were written to amuse us.

But there is one great treasure-hunt that is real. It has been going on for thousands of years, and will continue as long as men live. Hundreds of thousands of people have taken part in it directly. All of us have benefited from it indirectly. This real treasure-hunt is the search for the mineral riches hidden in the ground. No pirates put them there. Nature itself collected them and stored them in special hiding places. Like the pirates in the stories, nature left messages in code to guide us to the treasure. These messages are written in the rocks. People who study rocks and minerals learn this code. They can read the stories in the rocks and find out where to look for the treasure.

PRECIOUS PEBBLES

The beautiful diamond that flashes and glitters from its setting in a ring, brooch, or crown didn't always look so handsome. It had to be cut and polished by a jeweler to bring out its full beauty. Before it was cut it looked like a pebble. This is hardly surprising, because *it really was a pebble*. Diamonds, rubies, sapphires, and some of the other precious stones are pebbles of a special kind. They aren't found everywhere, but they are found in places where it is natural for pebbles to be.

THE DIAMONDS OF SINDBAD

One of the fascinating stories in the *Arabian Nights* is the tale about the second voyage of Sindbad, the merchant sailor. Sindbad and his fellow merchants were sailing from port to port to sell their goods. Their ship stopped at an island that was rich with beautiful trees and flowers, luscious fruits, and singing birds. Although there were no people on the island, the merchants and sailors landed, and walked about to enjoy the scenery. Sindbad fell asleep on the island and was left behind when the ship sailed on. He escaped from the island by tying himself to the leg of a roc, a giant bird that was believed to

133

feed elephants to its young. The roc, serving as a living helicopter, carried him from the island to a valley surrounded by high mountains. Here Sindbad found the ground covered with diamonds. At the top of the mountains, diamond merchants were gathering the diamonds without even going down into the valley. They slaughtered sheep, skinned them, and cut them into pieces. Then they threw the pieces of meat into the valley. When the meat fell on the pebbles that covered the ground, the diamonds stuck to the sticky blood. Later, eagles swooped down and carried the meat to their nests on the mountaintops. Then the merchants frightened the eagles away and picked the diamonds off the meat. Sindbad covered himself with one of these chunks of meat and was carried out of the valley by an eagle. Two things in this very exciting story are true. Diamonds are found in gravel beds in some mountainous regions. Also, diamonds do cling to thick sticky fluids. This property

134

can be used to separate diamonds from other pebbles.

Diamonds, rubies, sapphires, and some other gem stones are formed as crystals in some rock. Weathering of the rock frees them, and flowing water carries them into the valley. The gem stones are very hard, so they aren't worn down much by the rubbing they get as the water carries them. They are heavy, so they settle with other pebbles where the streams begin to slow down. In this way, flowing water acts as a collector of precious stones. It seeks them out in their scattered hiding places in the rocks, frees them, carries them off, and piles them up in beds of gravel. Gravel beds and beaches where valuable minerals are brought and dropped by moving water are called *placer deposits*.

THE HARDEST MINERAL

Diamond is the hardest substance there is. Because

of its great hardness, it is not only a gem stone, used as a decoration. It has important uses in industry. It serves as the teeth of cutting tools, like drills that must cut through rock or metal. Tiny chips of diamond are also used as phonograph needles. Because they are so hard, they can be used for a long time without wearing out.

A diamond, like the coal we burn in furnaces, and the graphite in our pencils, is made of carbon. It is harder and heavier than coal and graphite because it has a lot of carbon packed into a small space. It is interesting that while carbon in diamond is the hardest mineral, carbon in graphite is the softest. In fact, graphite is so soft that it is often used as a lubricant instead of oil.

WHERE DIAMONDS WERE BORN

For many centuries diamonds were found only in India and Borneo. After 1725, important diamond deposits were found in other countries as well. Today diamond fields are worked in Brazil, South Africa, British Guiana, and some other places.

The first diamond fields that were worked were gravel beds where the diamonds had been dropped by flowing water. The water brought them from high places where the rock that contained the diamonds had crumbled. In India and Brazil this rock turned out to be conglomerate formed from gravel beds that had piled up in past ages. The rock from which these old gravel beds came was nowhere to be seen. It had been completely destroyed by weathering long before any men were there to poke around among the rocks. The birthplace of diamonds was hidden from man's view by millions of years of time.

In South Africa, too, the first diamond fields found were gravel beds. But here, at last, the birthplace of diamonds was found, deep in the ground. Millions of years ago magma had risen under the ground and had hardened to form vertical "pipes" of rock. This igneous rock, known as *blue ground,* is a kind of *peridotite,* the type of rock found in the earth's mantle. When the magma hardened, crystals of diamond were formed in it. In India and Brazil these pipes of rock were destroyed long ago by weathering. But in South Africa many of them are still found in the ground. Now diamonds are dug from these pipes of "blue ground" in great mines.

THE DIAMOND MINES OF SOUTH AFRICA

More than half of the diamonds produced each year come from the diamond mines of South Africa. Some of these mines are "open pits." These are great holes in the ground that grow larger as the "blue ground" is removed. Others are underground mines reached by tunnels. Diamonds have been mined as deep as 3,600 feet under the ground.

The great Premier mine near Pretoria is an open pit. It is already about 700 feet deep. The rock is blasted in the ground, and the broken pieces are carted out of the hole. At the surface the diamonds are removed from the rock by a series of steps that imitate nature's way of doing it. First the rock is crushed. This takes the place of weathering. Then the crushed rock is washed with water in big washing pans. The water in the washing pans, like the water in streams that build up placer deposits, removes the mud and light rock, and leaves the diamonds and other heavy stones behind. The gravel that remains is carried by another stream of water across a table covered with grease. Here the diamonds are separated from the other heavy stones. The diamonds stick to the grease the way they stuck to the bloody meat in Sindbad's story. The other minerals slide over the grease and are carried away.

At Kimberley, in South Africa, there is an old abandoned open-pit mine. The hole in the ground is 1,500 feet wide and 1,300 feet deep. Water draining into the hole has made a "pond" 400 feet deep.

THE LARGEST DIAMOND

Imagine a diamond twice as big as your fist! This was the size of the Cullinan diamond, the largest ever found, when it was taken out of the Premier mine on January 25, 1905. It was 4 inches long, 2½ inches wide, and 2 inches thick, and weighed 1⅓ pounds. The South African government bought it as a gift for King Edward VII of England. The Cullinan diamond was cut into 9 large and 96 small gems. The largest of these is known as the *Star of South Africa.*

THE MOUNTAIN OF LIGHT

The most famous of all diamonds is the *Koh-i-Noor,* or Mountain of Light. According to the legends of India, it was worn by the hero Karna about five thousand years ago. Its recent history has been traced back about six hundred years. Rajahs and sultans kept taking it away from one another until the

140

year 1849. At that time the East India Company got it and gave it to Queen Victoria of England. It was recut and set in the Queen's crown.

MAN-MADE DIAMONDS

Diamonds are scarce and expensive. But they are made out of carbon, which is common and cheap. Ever since this fact was discovered by a British scientist in 1797, men have dreamed of making diamonds out of the softer, cheaper forms of carbon. They thought they might do it by squeezing the carbon at a high pressure and temperature. In 1890 the French scientist Moissan tried to make diamonds by melting a mixture of iron and graphite, and then cooling the mixture suddenly with water. He hoped that diamonds would form when the iron hardened, just as they had formed when magma hardened in the "blue ground" pipes of South Africa. He dissolved the solid iron, and found small crystals, some of which, he said, were real diamonds. It turned out later that he had been fooled by one of his assistants. The assistant didn't want the old man to be disappointed, so he had put a few real diamonds into the mixture while his chief was not looking. Moissan's method failed because the pressure and temperature he produced were not high enough.

In 1955, scientists working for the General Electric Company finally succeeded in making real diamonds. They used a special press that squeezed graphite with a pressure of 1½ million pounds per square inch, while the temperature was over 5,000 degrees Fahrenheit. The high pressure and temperature imitated the conditions found in the earth's mantle 240 miles under the ground. Their method works every time it is used. The largest diamond made so far is one sixteenth of an inch long. When the scientists learn how to make them larger and more cheaply, man-made diamonds will work side by side with natural diamonds in the cutting tools of industry.

RUBY AND SAPPHIRE

Most rubies and sapphires, like diamonds, were born as crystals in cooling magma. Some were formed in peridotite; others took shape in pegmatite. They were freed from the rocks by weathering and dropped by streams in beds of gravel.

The best rubies come from Burma. These were formed from *mud,* millions of years ago. The mud was mixed with limestone that was changed by heat and pressure deep under the ground. The limestone became marble, and the mud became rubies. Later, weathering freed the rubies from the marble. Now they lie in the gravel beds of streams. Rubies are found in the United States, too, in North Carolina.

Ruby and sapphire are relatives of *emery,* which is used in emery wheels and emery cloth for grinding. All three are crystals of the same mineral, *corundum.* Only their colors are different. Ruby is red, sapphire is blue, and emery is black. Corundum is next in

143

hardness to diamond. It is number 9 in the scale of hardness.

The chemical in corundum is burnt aluminum, and is called *alumina*. Powdered alumina is made very easily. If ammonia water is mixed with alum dissolved in water, a jelly is formed. This jelly is made up of alumina combined with water. If the jelly is heated to drive out the water, the powdered alumina remains. Artificial rubies and sapphires are now made from this powder. They are just as good as those found in nature.

Because of their hardness, rubies and sapphires can be rubbed for a long time without being worn down. For this reason, tiny rubies and sapphires that aren't good enough to be used as gems are used as bearings in watches.

It is interesting that the jelly from which alumina is made is also used as a medicine. The same chemical may become a medicine for your stomach, a bearing in your watch, a gem stone in a brooch, or the grinding face of an emery wheel!

BERYL AND TOPAZ

Two other well-known gem stones are *emerald* and *aquamarine*. They are both forms of the same mineral, *beryl*, dressed up in different colors. When the beryl is grass-green, it is emerald. If it is blue-green or blue in color, it is aquamarine. Aquamarine is usually found in igneous rocks like pegmatite and granite. Emerald occurs in metamorphic rocks like mica schist and marble.

In 1910 a crystal of aquamarine weighing 243 pounds was found in Brazil. In 1928 a really gigantic crystal of beryl was found in pegmatite in Maine. The crystal was 18 feet long and 4 feet wide, and weighed 18 tons. It was not of gem quality.

Where you find beryl you may also find *topaz*. Topaz was formed in pegmatite or granite when vapors

145

or liquids that had escaped from hot magma combined with the feldspar in the rock. Topaz may have many different colors, or no color at all. It is number 8 in the scale of hardness.

GOLD

When magma breaks into an old rock to form a dike or sill, it may come up mixed with hot water. Hot water that flows out of magma has minerals dissolved in it. When the water flows into cracks and cavities, the minerals, as the water cools, begin to form crystals. If the supply of dissolved minerals is big enough, the crystals grow until the crack or cavity is filled. A completely filled crack becomes a *vein*. Near some igneous rocks there are veins made up of quartz with particles of gold in it. These are the veins that gold prospectors look for.

If air and water, those old enemies of rock, get at the vein before the gold prospectors do, then the

146

rock is weathered. It crumbles, and its fragments are carried away by flowing water. As gold resists weathering, and is heavy, it piles up in the stream beds with the sand and gravel in placer deposits. This gives the prospectors another chance to get at the gold. They "pan" the sand and gravel of the stream. They wash away the lightweight mud and stone, to separate them from the heavy gold.

Most of the gold that is found consists of small grains. It takes much work to find the grains and separate them from the rock or gravel. That is why gold is so expensive. But sometimes prospectors and miners come across lumps or *nuggets* of gold. When gold was discovered in California, Australia, and Alaska, people rushed to these places hoping to become rich. They knew they had difficult days of hard work ahead of them, but they all hoped to make a lucky find of a rich vein or a large nugget. The largest gold nugget ever discovered was found at Hill

End, in New South Wales, Australia. It was 4 feet 9 inches long, 3 feet 3 inches wide, and about 4 inches thick. It was sold for $148,000.

THE OLIVER MARTIN NUGGET

In the year 1854, death and the floods that build placer deposits led Oliver Martin to an eighty-pound gold nugget in California. Oliver Martin and his friend John Fowler were traveling across gold-mining territory. Night overtook them on November 17, just as they came upon a deserted shack built by prospectors during the gold rush of 1848. The shack was in a narrow canyon that had steep sides. During the night, it began to rain. Water poured out of the sky in torrents. Streams flowing down from the heights began to fill the canyon. Martin and Fowler were awakened when the water streamed into the cabin. They rushed outside and tried to climb out of the canyon to escape the flood. But the wall of the canyon was too steep. Water cascading down the wall swept them back. The raging flood knocked them down and carried them downstream. Fowler was drowned. Martin was swept into the branches of an oak tree, where he managed to hold on. The next day, when the flood was over, Martin had the sad duty of burying his friend. He got a pick and shovel and began to dig in the sand that had been piled up by the fatal flood and many floods before it. Two feet under the ground his shovel struck the gold nugget.

Martin took his nugget on a tour of the country. People paid money to see the nugget and hear his story. After taking in $10,000 in this way, he sold the nugget for $22,700.

PROSPECTING IN A FACTORY

Large amounts of gold are used today to make pen points for fountain pens. When the points are ground and polished, gold dust is rubbed off. The dust floats in the air, falls on the clothing of the

149

workers, and settles on the floor. This dust is valuable, so the manufacturers do all they can to get it back. They filter the air. They wash the clothes of the workers, and then filter the wash water. They burn floor sweepings, rags and paper, and worn-out shoes. Then they "pan" the ashes. By all these means they recover over a million dollars' worth of gold dust each year.

TREASURES THAT DON'T GLITTER

Gold and sparkling jewels are the least important of the treasures we dig out of the ground. We get more value out of other minerals that aren't as pretty, but have many uses in everyday life. We use rocks to make the cement and lime that go into the walls of our buildings. We use clay to make pottery and bricks. We use sand to make glass. We use gravel to make roadbeds and concrete. But most important of all are the minerals from which we get our metals, and the mineral fuels that keep our fires burning.

IRON

The most important of the metals we use is *iron*. But iron is rarely found as a metal in nature. It is usually hidden in some mineral, combined with other chemicals. When we *smelt* the mineral in a furnace, chemical action separates the iron from the other chemicals. A mineral from which we remove a metal is called an *ore*. The chief ores from which we get iron are *hematite* and *limonite*. Hematite is the red rust of iron, in which iron is combined with oxygen. Limonite, which gives most clay its yellow color, is iron rust combined with water.

In the United States large amounts of hematite and limonite are dug out of open pits in the Lake Superior district. The deep beds of iron ore that are there were built up by water. Millions of years ago

151

that part of the continent was covered by shallow seas. Tiny plants living in the water made iron compounds settle out of the water. The iron compounds were mixed with quartz crystals that were piling up to form chert and jasper. Later the sea floor rose, the seas drained away, and the beds became dry land. Rain over the land soaked into the ground, and water seeped through the mineral mixture. First the water changed the iron compounds into hematite and limonite. Then, as water continued to seep through, it slowly dissolved the chert and jasper, and carried them away. The hematite and limonite remained.

MAGNETIC SAND

Another important ore that contains iron is *magnetite*. It is one of the few minerals that can be attracted by a magnet. Some pieces of magnetite act as magnets themselves. These are called *loadstones*.

Magnetite is dark gray or black. Small crystals of

it are found in granite. Magnetite, like quartz, resists weathering. When the granite crumbles, while
the mica and feldspar rot, the magnetite grains, like
the quartz grains, remain and are carried away by
flowing water. That's why magnetite grains are found
in placer deposits, where they were dropped by the
water. The next time you are at the beach, examine
the sand carefully. You will see some black grains
mixed with the light-colored quartz in the sand.
Some of these grains are magnetite. You can separate them from the rest by passing a magnet through
the sand. The magnetite grains will jump up to the
magnet and cling to it.

FOOL'S GOLD

One of the interesting iron minerals is a compound of iron and sulphur called *pyrite*. It is also
called "fool's gold," because its brassy-yellow color
has misled many hopeful but inexperienced gold-
hunters. Two thousand years ago, pyrite was impor-

tant as a fire-maker. You can make a spark with pyrite by striking it with flint. Pyrite is not used as a source of iron. It is used to make sulphuric acid.

OTHER METAL ORES

Some of the other common metals that are important today are copper, lead, tin, zinc, and aluminum. You will find copper in a penny, lead and tin in solder, zinc in the jacket of a flashlight battery, and aluminum in a saucepan in your kitchen.

Most of the copper produced in the United States comes from a dark-gray mineral called *chalcocite*. It is a compound of copper and sulphur. Another common copper ore is *chalcopyrite,* in which copper and sulphur are combined with iron. Like pyrite, it has a brassy-yellow color. Lead is obtained from *galena,* a compound of lead and sulphur. Galena is silvery gray and shines like a metal. The chief ore of tin is *cassiterite* or tinstone, a compound of tin and oxygen. It resists weathering. So, like quartz, gold, and gem

154

stones, it piles up in river-bed gravels. We get zinc from *sphalerite,* a compound of zinc and sulphur. Aluminum comes from *bauxite,* in which it is combined with oxygen and water.

COAL

We use large amounts of power each year to light and heat our homes and to run the machinery in our factories. We get most of this power from minerals dug out of the ground. The power is hidden in *coal, oil,* and *natural gas.* We free it for use when we burn these minerals as fuel.

We get almost half of the power we use in the United States from coal. On page 76 we learned how coal was formed millions of years ago from buried plants. The wood in the plants was a combination of carbon and water. Chemical changes in the buried plants freed most of the carbon. The free carbon gives coal its black color.

Coal has many important uses. Some of it is burned

155

to heat our homes. Large amounts are burned, too, at electric power stations. There the heat released by the burning coal is used to make steam. The steam drives turbines, which are attached to dynamos. Then the turning dynamos generate the electric currents used in factories, offices, and homes. Some coal is *baked* to turn it into *coke*. Then the coke is used at the steel mills where iron ore is smelted. In an ore like hematite, the iron is a prisoner, held in a strong embrace by the oxygen with which it is combined. The coke takes the oxygen away from the iron, and so sets the iron free.

There is *tar* as well as free carbon in coal. When the coal is baked to make coke, the tar is separated from it. Many valuable products are made from this tar. By the magic of chemistry, the tar is turned into nylon, fertilizer, perfumes, sulfa drugs, rubber, dyes, vitamins, explosives, paint, and many other things.

156

ROCK OIL

The gasoline we burn in our automobile engines comes from *petroleum*. The word *petroleum* shows its mineral nature, because it means "rock oil." Like coal, petroleum is a mineral formed out of things that were once alive. Coal comes from plants that once grew in great swamps. Petroleum comes from tiny animals that once lived in the sea. When the animals died, they fell to the sea floor and became part of the sediment that was piling up there. While the rest of the sediment was turned into rocks like shale and sandstone, the partly rotted bodies of the animals were turned into oil and natural gas.

Oil wells are dug in places where the oil has collected in large pools under the ground. From long experience with oil pools, geologists now know how they were formed, and where they can expect to find them. The drawing on page 158 shows one way in

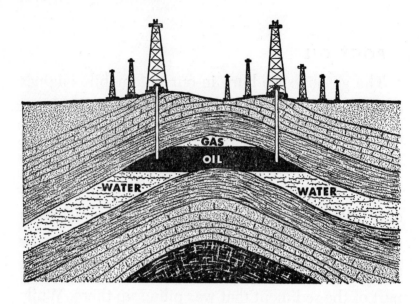

which an oil pool was formed. Oil and water filled
the tiny spaces between the grains of sand in a sandstone. The sandstone was sandwiched between layers of shale. A long time ago the rocks in the ground
were folded, forming a bump or "dome" in the rock.
Oil is lighter than water, so it floated up over the
water in the sandstone. It couldn't seep into the shale
above it, because shale is too tightly packed to let

158

the oil get in. So the oil was trapped right under the dome. The gas, being lighter than the oil, was trapped above the pool of oil.

ATOMIC ENERGY

A new fuel has begun to take its place alongside coal, oil, and natural gas. This new fuel is the fuel for atomic energy. It is a fuel that we do not burn. The energy we get from it is locked inside its atoms. We release the energy by splitting the atoms.

One of the fuels for atomic energy is *uranium*. Ordinary uranium is a mixture of two different kinds of uranium that have different weights. The lighter one, called Uranium 235, is the atomic fuel. To split atoms of Uranium 235, we fire special "bullets" at them. The bullets we use are slow-moving tiny particles called *neutrons*. Each atom that is split releases some energy, and also fires out a few fast-moving neutrons.

The fast-moving neutrons that are fired out of the

splitting atoms can be put to work. But first they have to be slowed down. This is done by surrounding the atomic fuel with special lightweight materials called *moderators*. When the neutrons are fired out of the splitting atoms in the fuel, they pass through the moderator, which slows them down. When they are slow enough, they can be used to split more atoms. One of the materials that can be used as a moderator is the lightweight metal *beryllium*.

Less than one part in a hundred of ordinary uranium is made up of Uranium 235. The rest of it is called Uranium 238. It is not an atomic fuel, because a slow neutron will not make it split. But *it can be used to make another atomic fuel*. When Uranium 238 is struck by a neutron, it is turned into a metal called *plutonium*. Plutonium, like Uranium 235, is an atomic fuel. So *all of uranium can be turned into a source of atomic energy*.

There is another metal that is not an atomic fuel, but can be turned into one. This metal is *thorium*.

160

When it is hit by a neutron, it turns into Uranium 233, which is an atomic fuel like Uranium 235.

The development of atomic energy has given new value to the metals uranium, thorium, and beryllium. A world-wide search is under way to find the minerals in which they are hidden.

URANIUM

Uranium is everywhere. It is found in nearly every type of rock. It is also in the water of the sea. In the earth's crust, on the average, there are two tenths of an ounce of uranium in every ton of rock. In the sea, there is seven hundredths of an ounce of uranium in every thousand tons of water. But these amounts are so small that it is impractical to try to remove the uranium from sea water or from most rocks. To get uranium we must find rocks that have a lot of uranium in a small space. Rocks like these serve as *uranium ores* from which we can remove the uranium without too much work or expense.

Uranium is never found as a free metal. It is always found combined with other elements. It occurs in more than one hundred and fifty minerals. But only a few of them are valuable as ores from which uranium can be removed. The two most important uranium ores are *pitchblende* and *carnotite*.

Pitchblende is found in irregular rounded masses, usually laid down in layers. Its hardness is between 5 and 6. It is grayish black, shines like pitch, and has a black streak. More than half of pitchblende ore is uranium. Pitchblende deposits were built up when hot water flowed out of magma under the ground and seeped into cracks in the surrounding rock. As the water cooled, the pitchblende, mixed with quartz, calcite, or dolomite, settled out of the water and filled the cracks to form veins in the rock. Pitchblende is most likely to be found where metals like iron, copper, cobalt, lead, silver, and bismuth are located. The largest deposits of pitchblende are found in the Belgian Congo, in the Northwest Territories of Canada, and in Czechoslovakia. In the United States there is pitchblende in Utah and Arizona.

When pitchblende occurs in crystal form, it is called *uraninite*. Uraninite crystals are found in some pegmatites. Usually there aren't enough of the crystals in the pegmatite to make it worth while to remove them. But if the pegmatite is quarried for some other purpose, the uraninite may be obtained as a by-product.

Another uranium mineral that occurs in veins is *davidite*. It is dark brown or black. Some deposits have a glassy shine, while others shine almost like a metal. Veins of davidite were found in gneiss and schist in Radium Hill, an old radium mine in Australia.

When pitchblende, uraninite, and davidite are exposed to the air, they begin to weather. The chemical action of weathering changes them into other minerals, whose colors are bright yellow, orange, and green. The weathered parts are powdery, or consist of fine needles and flakes. Uranium prospectors always investigate a crumbly rock that is brightly colored, because it may be the top of a uranium deposit.

After uranium minerals have weathered, rain water dissolves them and carries them away. Then it may drop them in flat layers in sedimentary rocks. This is how the *carnotite* deposits of Colorado, Utah, Arizona, and New Mexico were built up. Carnotite has a lemon-yellow color, a yellow streak, and an earthy luster. It is soft enough to be scratched with your fingernail. It may be found in sandstone, often in the company of petrified wood.

Another uranium mineral, closely related to carnotite, is *tyuyamunite*. It gets its strange-sounding name from the town of Tyuya Muyun in Turkistan. It is more green in color than carnotite, and is found in limestone and dolomite instead of sandstone. In the United States it has been found in New Mexico and Utah.

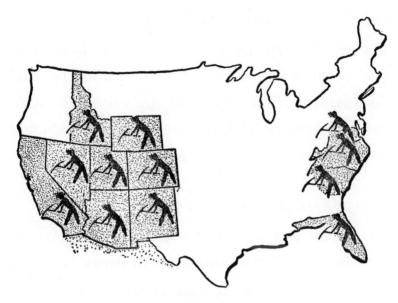

Areas of the United States where uranium
ores have been found

Several other uranium ores are also found in the
United States. *Torbernite* and *meta-torbernite* have
a bright emerald color and a pearly luster. They
occur in flat square cystals through which light can
pass. They can be scratched by your fingernail. Deposits have been found in Utah and Arizona. *Autunite* and *meta-autunite* are somewhat like torbernite.

165

They are lemon or sulphur yellow, and are found in igneous rocks in dry regions. Deposits have been located in Utah, New Mexico, California, and Nevada. *Uranophane* has a lighter color than autunite, and is found in limestone in New Mexico and Wyoming.

RADIATION DETECTORS

Uranium is a *radio-active* element. That means that some of its atoms break up or decay by themselves. We have already seen how the decay of uranium turns it into a clock for measuring the ages of rocks. This decay is also useful to prospectors, because *it helps them locate deposits of uranium ores.* Each atom that decays sends out some tiny particles. The particles are invisible, but they can be detected by two special instruments. One of them is the *Geiger counter*. In a Geiger counter the particles are caught in a tube filled with gas. When a particle bumps into a molecule of the gas, it starts an electric

166

current. Then the electric current makes a click in headphones, or flashes a neon lamp, or moves the pointer on a dial. In a large deposit of uranium, there are many atoms decaying. So, near a uranium ore, a Geiger counter is bombarded by a lot of particles, one after another.

The other instrument that can detect these particles is a *scintillation counter.* In this instrument the particles are caught on a crystal that sends out a tiny flash of light every time a particle hits it. A photo-multiplier tube "sees" each flash of light and turns it into an electric current.

There are three types of particles fired out of decaying uranium atoms. They are called alpha, beta, and gamma rays. Alpha and beta rays are easy to stop, so they don't travel very far. But gamma rays are like X-rays. They can pass through a foot of rock, two and one-half feet of water, or several hundred feet of air before they are stopped. In 1950, a deposit of carnotite was discovered at Powder

167

River, Wyoming, when gamma rays from the deposit reached a Geiger counter in an airplane several hundred feet up in the air.

THORIUM

Thorium, like Uranium 238, can be turned into an atomic fuel. It occurs in about one hundred minerals, but only one of them is useful as an ore. This mineral is called *monazite*. Monazite occurs in small amounts in pegmatite and granite. The amount is so small that it doesn't pay to try to remove it from these rocks. But nature removes it for us, free of charge. When granite weathers, it crumbles. But monazite resists weathering, so the grains of monazite remain. Then they are carried away by flowing water and are dropped in placer deposits along rivers and beaches. Monazite is usually found together with a black mineral called *ilmenite,* so *black sand* may be a sign of monazite. There are large black-sand monazite deposits on beaches in India and

Brazil. In the United States, monazite has been found in Florida, North and South Carolina, Idaho, California, Montana, Virginia, and Nevada.

Monazite sand is made up of small, round glassy grains that may be yellow-brown, yellow, or honey-yellow. They have a pale-brown streak. The hardness is 5 to 5½.

BERYLLIUM

Beryllium is important as a *moderator* in atomic power plants. The only important ore from which beryllium is obtained is the mineral *beryl*. Beryl has already been described as a precious stone. Crystals of beryl are found in pegmatite. Green beryl of gem quality is called *emerald*. Blue beryl is called *aquamarine*. But not all crystals of beryl are of gem quality. Those that are not useful to the jeweler are useful to the atomic-energy engineer. The beryllium that is extracted from them can be used as a moderator for slowing down fast-moving neutrons.

169

Starting a Collection

MANY people have fun collecting rocks and minerals. If you want to join in the fun, start a collection of your own.

THE TOOLS YOU NEED

You need only a few tools to work with when you start collecting rocks and minerals. Here is a list of them:

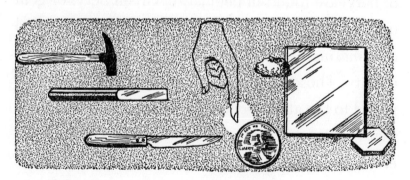

1. A hammer and a cold chisel, for breaking off specimens.

2. A kit for testing hardness. You can start by using your fingernail, a copper penny, a knife, a flat piece of glass, and a piece of quartz.

3. A tile for getting the streak of minerals.

4. A magnifying glass.

5. A bottle of vinegar.

6. A canvas bag with a shoulder strap; sheets of newspaper; and paper bags. These are for collecting trips.

7. A notebook, pencil, and adhesive tape, for keeping records.

171

8. Egg-boxes and jars for storage.

WHERE TO BEGIN

Begin at home. Get samples of the different rocks and minerals in your neighborhood.

A COLLECTING TRIP

You can turn every hike into a collecting trip. To prepare for it, do these things first:

Cut a strip of adhesive tape into small pieces. Then use pen and ink to write numbers on them: 1, 2, 3, and so on. Mount them on a piece of wax paper.

Now put these things into your canvas bag: the hammer and chisel; the pencil and notebook; the pieces of adhesive tape; the sheets of newspaper and paper bags; your lunch, if you expect to be out past lunch time.

On the trip, watch for interesting specimens. Get samples of the pebbles along roads and streams, and the gravel in roadbeds. Examine cliffs and large rocks to see if you can recognize the flakes of schist, the dark and light bands of gneiss, the layers of shale, or the graininess of sandstone. Look for places where magma may have broken into a rock to form a dike of igneous rock. Chip off pieces with your hammer and chisel.

Every time you take a specimen, stick one of the numbered pieces of adhesive tape on it. Write the number in your notebook, and, next to the number, describe in a few words the place where you found it. Then wrap the specimen in a piece of newspaper and put it in your canvas bag. If you find interesting specimens of sand or clay, put samples into the paper bags, and number them in the same way.

TESTING YOUR FINDS

When you get home, try to identify the specimens you brought back. Examine the color and the streak of minerals. Test them for hardness. Use the vinegar test if you think you have calcite. Watch for signs of crystal shape. Notice how the minerals break. Compare the appearance of rocks with descriptions and pictures in this book and other books about rocks and minerals. When you have identified a specimen, write its name next to its number in your notebook. Store stones in the egg-boxes, using one compartment for each stone. Keep sands, clays, and small crystals in jars.

LEARN AS YOU COLLECT

If you enjoy collecting stones and want to continue it as a hobby, you will want to learn more about rocks and minerals. You will find helpful pictures and descriptions in these books: *The Rock Book,* by Carroll Lane Fenton and Mildred Adams Fenton, published by Doubleday & Company, Inc.; and *Field Book of Common Rocks and Minerals,* by F. B. Loomis, published by G. P. Putnam's Sons. Your librarian can suggest other books, too.

Your local natural-history museum may have a

collection of rocks and minerals on display. Visit the museum, and study the display. It will help you identify the rocks and minerals you collect.

WHEN YOU TRAVEL

You can add to your collection when you go on trips. Specimens will be easy to get where a road has been cut through a hill. If you pass near quarries and mines, visit them. You may be permitted to take samples of rocks and ores.

WHERE TO BUY

You can buy excellent samples of rocks and minerals, at low cost, from Ward's Natural Science Establishment, Beechwood Station, Rochester, New York. Send for their catalogue. If you don't travel much, this is a good way to get specimens from other parts of the country. They are already correctly labeled, so they will help you learn how to recognize the different rocks and minerals.

175

Index

[*The number 86 in italics refers to the group of photographs inserted after page 86.*]

i

A NOTE ON THE

TYPE

IN WHICH THIS BOOK IS SET

THE TEXT *of this book is set in Caledonia, a Linotype face designed by* W. A. DWIGGINS. *It belongs to the family of printing types called "modern face" by printers—a term used to mark the change in style of type-letters that occurred about 1800. Caledonia borders on the general design of Scotch Modern, but is more freely drawn than that letter.*

THE BOOK *was composed, printed, and bound by* H. WOLFF, *New York. Paper made by* P. H. GLATFELTER CO., *Spring Grove, Pa. Typography by* CHARLES FARRELL.

3455